W9-AAM-702

Teaching Second Grade

By Valerie SchifferDanoff

SCHOLASTIC
PROFESSIONAL BOOKS

NEW YORK • TORONTO • LONDON • AUCKLAND • SYDNEY
MEXICO CITY • NEW DELHI • HONG KONG

Dedicated to my son, Joshua Mattey,
in celebration of his educational achievement on May 9, 1998

I'd like to acknowledge Jill Lieberman for her over 28 years of teaching
and especially for making second grade look like so much fun that I just had to try it.
She has been an inspiration and a mentor.

Scholastic Inc. grants teachers permission to photocopy the activity sheets from this book for classroom use. No other part of this publication may be reproduced in whole or in part, or stored in a retrieval system, or transmitted in any form or by any means electronic or mechanical, photocopying, recording, or otherwise, without written permission of the publisher. For information regarding permission, write to Scholastic, Inc. 555 Broadway, New York, NY 10012.

Cover design by Jaime Lucero and Pamela Simmons
Interior design by Solutions by Design, Inc.
Interior Illustrations by Norma Ortiz
Cover photograph by Jim Cummins/FPG
Interior photographs by Saul Danoff and Valerie SchifferDanoff

ISBN 0-590-22180-9

Copyright © 2000 by Valerie SchifferDanoff

Printed In the U.S.A. All rights reserved.

Table of Contents

Introduction

During the past 15 years I've taught prekindergarten, kindergarten, first grade, second grade, and special education. Over the years, I've seen changes in philosophy and materials at each level of teaching. When I moved from prekindergarten to kindergarten, there was a flurry of interest in hands-on teaching. When I went from kindergarten to first grade, the big interest was in using literature to teach reading. Since I moved from first grade to second grade recently, the trend has been toward going back to the basics. Yet constant throughout the years has been the need to search for the techniques and materials that would bring out the best of my teaching talents while encouraging the depth and breadth of learning for each of my students.

As I moved through philosophies and grades, I gathered and created materials, learned new techniques and fine-tuned old ones, and wrote four books. After I'd taught first grade for eight years—bringing children to a certain stage in reading and writing—I wanted to see what happens next. I was curious. So, after researching, creating, designing, organizing, structuring, and gathering materials, I was ready to advance with my students—to second grade. This book was inspired by that move.

The book is organized around questions you may have, whether you're just beginning to teach, just beginning to teach second grade, or are interested in discovering new activities and ideas from another veteran teacher.

So enjoy as I have and, along with me, help your second graders build on all their prior learning and experiences.

CHAPTER 1

What to Expect in Second Grade

What is second grade really like? Second grade is fun! The children have been in school for two years. They know the school routine. They have friends. Best of all, at least half of your class may be fairly fluent readers. You have the fun of expanding their horizons and capitalizing on their eagerness to learn. For example, when you write something on the board or on a chart, you experience the joy of seeing the children read it—almost eat it up—as you write. The children have the fun of exploring, expanding, and extending their skills and abilities without too much struggle. That initial risk taking required of beginning readers has become a strength they can transfer to more learning. This chapter will establish some general expectations of second graders.

What are second graders like?

Second graders

- are anxious to read chapter books.
- are ready to read chapter books.
- love listening to chapter books.
- are beginning to be writers.
- like to write and go on and on and on and on and on and on....
- are beginning to write dialogue and love to mimic daily talk.
- want to know how to tell time.
- can begin to question on their own.
- love poetry.
- have a sense of humor.
- like to prove how smart they are.
- are ready to learn and apply manners.
- bicker/argue.
- are ready to discuss and reason about disputes, especially those that occurred on the playground during recess.

Where did they leave off?

It's important to remember that, just like any other grade, second graders return to school not remembering where they left off. It's also important to remember that early in the year you're teaching first graders who are beginning second grade. They've acquired skills but haven't had much of a chance to use and enjoy using them. The fun of putting newly acquired skills to use is what second grade is all about. To quote my students from the first week of school, "This is much more fun than first grade!"

Where did they leave off in reading?

First grade is a feverish, pressure-filled, high-energy year for students and teachers alike. Expectations are high for the students to learn to read and write. Children and parents worry about who's reading what. Although previous exposure and daily practice are important, each child's ability to learn to read and write is developmental as well as environmental. Being ready is critical. By second grade, more children are ready.

There's a range of abilities in second grade, but the gap closes a little faster than it did earlier. Some children are fairly fluent readers. Some have just gained fluency. Some children have acquired the knowledge needed to begin reading. Some need more exposure to cues and strategies. You can use last year's records to determine the range of your students' abilities before the first day of school or use the suggestions for assessment on page 43.

What are they ready to read?

If they haven't read much over the summer, your students may be afraid to try it at first. You may even have to remind them that they know how to read. If they left first grade having struggled with reading and aren't reading yet, they're probably even more fearful now. However, they may be ready to try a low- to medium-text chapter book if they were reading fairly fluently in first grade, have practiced over the summer, and still enjoy a great picture book. (See student book lists on page 33.) And all students still need phonics cues for decoding new vocabulary, and need to be reminded of this. (For more on reading, see page 41.)

What can second graders be expected to spell?

It's important to remember that most second graders are moving away from phonetic spelling, going beyond transitional spelling, and are much more aware of correct spelling. A second grader will ask, "Is that how you *really* spell it?" much more frequently than a first grader. This means your students can decode and learn new vocabulary more rapidly. (For more on spelling, see page 73.)

What are second graders ready to write?

Most second graders have acquired some written-language skills. They are now ready to explore its many facets comfortably and confidently. Various writing experiences heighten interest, allow for individual development, and provide exciting accomplishments for the whole class.

Writing workshops with mini-lessons enable second-grade writers to learn while using what they already know. However, even if they left first grade writing a "whole story," be prepared for those fluent writers to feel that five sentences tell it all. Practicing writing over the summer is rare. Therefore, it's helpful to get students started with a few writing projects that incorporate some basic mini-lessons and journal ideas. (For details on writing, see page 53.)

What about rules?

Rules really were meant to be broken. That's why posting them at the beginning of second grade may not be such a good idea, especially if you're the one who may need to break one. I've found it's best to cite rules as situations arise. Otherwise you may find yourself providing unnecessary information. For example, in response to, "He cut me off!," simply saying, "It's not polite to step in front of someone in line," at the time it occurs serves the same purpose as posting it as a rule. That way, if you see the need to move a person from one place in line to another, you won't hear a typical second-grade reaction like, "It's a rule that there's no cutting!" Because, as mentioned earlier, second graders like to prove how smart they are.

Are second graders ready for homework?

Yes, they are ready, willing, and able to take home and complete a homework assignment. Have your students write the assignment down. (You will find a Homework Assignment Sheet on page 11.) Encourage parents to be aware of assignments and to set aside a time and space for their child to complete homework.

Writing a letter to parents about homework and homework requirements or discussing it on parents' night and during report-card conferences is also helpful.

What kind of homework can second graders do?

Second graders, like children at all grade levels, can work at home on reinforcing skills taught in school. The chapters that follow, on math, spelling, reading, and writing, include specific homework possibilities and suggestions. Also, look at grade-level workbooks for possibilities, and consider creating some teacher-made materials of your own. In this book, Ⓗ indicates homework suggestions.

What's a good way to check homework?

Homework can be collected daily. A checklist may be useful. Time can be set aside each day to have children self-correct math. I've found it's most effective for second graders to have their homework corrected as soon as possible. I collect and return some homework, like spelling journals, daily. Other homework, like creative writing, may be kept for a day or two.

What is a good way to celebrate second graders' birthdays?

Birthdays are special, and second graders love to be acknowledged. Have each child write the birthday child a letter about how special he or she is

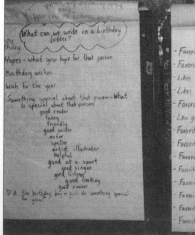

along with birthday wishes. To help the letter writers address specifics, have the birthday child answer questions about his or her favorite things, and write them on a chart.

Have a chart of birthday sayings available, too. Place the letters in a special envelope or folder that the birthday child can decorate while classmates are writing the letters.

Letter 1 (acrostic HAPPY BIRTHDAY):

Dear Sam,

H
A
P — Happy happy happy birthday!! The color green is very
P — nice! What does it remind you of? What is your favorite candy? The round-up is
Y — a SUPER SUPER ride! A monkey is funny a
B — little like how you are funny sometimes. The Mississippi river
I — is a nice river! The Simpsons is a GREAT
R — GREAT GREAT t.v.
T — show!! You're already
H — 8! Wow! Wow! Wow!! I hope you have a
D — very very good, fourth! Enjoy your...
a — CONG...
y

Letter 2 (Charlie's letter):

Dear Sam,
Happy Birthday!! Congratulations! You're eight years old now! I hope you have a great time! The round-up is such a fun and scary ride to go on. You must be pretty brave to go on it! You must be cool because you like the Simpsons. Monkeys are great to like because they do really funny things. You had a great idea to name our frog Mitchell. You're a great kid!

Your Friend
Charlie

P.S. Alan Houston is an awesome basketball player

Knicks Pacers
112

Letter 3 (Mrs. Danoff):

... a very interesting story too. Keep learning and expressing yourself so well.

Love,
Mrs. Danoff

Letter 4:

May 15, 1998

Dear Sam,

Happy Eighth Birthday! We have had a fun and ... year together. I am ... to have had the ... ty to get to know you. ... lly appreciate your ... humor. You've learned ... are it at the right ... whole class can enjoy ... What a great ... e. You can write

---

Mrs. Danoff's Birthday Story

It's summer now. I am writing about what I plan to do this coming year, because I haven't done it yet. That is what those of you who have summer birthdays will have to do.

My birthday is always on a holiday. That's because I was born on Valentine's Day. I really love my birthday. Actually, I think everybody's birthday is its own special holiday.

I am making big plans, though, because this is a big birthday for me. I am planning to celebrate five decades, or fifty years, or half a century of Valentine birthdays. I am going to have a big party and invite all my friends. I am really hoping that my sons will be able to come home from college and join in the celebration. I hope their girlfriends will join us, too. The party will be at my house. The theme will be valentines. I'll have a heart-shaped cake, heart-shaped cookies, and a valentine for everyone. I'll serve dinner, of course, too.

Now you may be wondering, "What do adults do at a party?" Well, it's true, we don't usually have a magician or play games. So what will we do at the party? We'll eat, listen and talk to each other, play music, and mostly relax with friends. Adults like to laugh, just like children do. So we'll tell jokes, too. I am hoping that each person will tell his or her own story of how we came to know each other. Since it is Valentine's Day, I hope everybody will bring his or her own special feeling about love and friendship as well.

Then, guess what I'll have to do…I'll have to clean up! But it will have been fun celebrating with my family and friends.

One activity that has been especially successful is a birthday writing package we call the Birthday Box that the birthday girl or boy takes home. The package includes a book with birthday stories (*One-Minute Birthday Stories* by Shari Lewis, for example), a class birthday journal, and directions. The birthday child reads a birthday story with or to a parent and then writes in the class birthday journal about his or her birthday celebration. Lewis's stories can serve as a model. Including a story about your own birthday can be a model, too. Remember to make allowances for summer birthdays. Summer birthday children can write about their plans.

Also, at the beginning of the year, I send out two letters regarding birthday celebrations.

Bedford Village Elementary School

Dear Parents,

Story Snack can be a wonderful experience for you, your child, and our class. The idea is to read a book and bring a simple, finger food snack that is related to a character or idea in the story. One year a parent read a story about a rabbit. She and her son prepared a simple snack made from a rice cake, peanut butter and celery sticks. She arranged the items on a plate to look like a rabbit.

I invite you or a grandparent to share a **Story Snack** with our class this year. You can either choose a book at home with your child or I can help with a suggestion. You may want to choose to make a special or traditional family recipe and read a book related to this; or read a birthday book to celebrate your child's birthday and share a birthday snack. Otherwise, birthdays are celebrated by your simply sending in a snack on or close to your child's birthday. Summer birthdays are celebrated in June.

I hope that you can share a **Story Snack** one time this year. Please send a note in with your child about two weeks prior to the time and day you would like to come. I will get back to you as soon as possible to confirm the date.

I look forward to meeting you and sharing a happy new school year.

Regards,

Bedford Village Elementary School

Dear Parents and Children:

During the school year I will be sending home a special story writing package. It is a birthday box. You will need to allow about 30 minutes of home time to complete it.

The birthday box will be sent home the day after your birthday or as close to that day a possible. A special birthday book, a writing experience and instructions for your entry are in the box. Allowances will be made for vacations and summer birthdays.

When the box is returned to school the following day, your child will have the opportunity to share his or her birthday entry with our class.

Regards,

Valerie Schifferdaroff

The following chapters describe second graders' learning development along with successful methods and materials to teach them.

Homework for the Week of_____

Homework Assignment Sheet

You are expected to read for at least 15 minutes every night and to study your math facts.

....

MONDAY   **Spelling:** Write the words on the list and the word-sort words in A–Z order.

Math:_____

Writing:_____

Remember: _____

....

TUESDAY   **Spelling:** Write 4 sentences using words 1–4 on the list.

Math:_____

Writing:_____

Remember: _____

....

WEDNESDAY   **Spelling:** Write 4 sentences using words 5–8 on the list.

Math:_____

Writing:_____

Remember: _____

....

THURSDAY   **Spelling:** Study all the words listed for the week, or write 4 sentences using 4 word-sort words.

Math:_____

Writing:_____

Remember: _____

CHAPTER 2

Preparing to Teach Second Grade

Now that you have an idea of what second graders are bringing with them, it's time to ask yourself what you can bring to this age level. What can you prepare ahead of time? How can you best support the children's needs, encourage their growth, teach them second-grade skills, and have fun, too? Hopefully, you'll find many of the answers within the pages of this book. So read on!

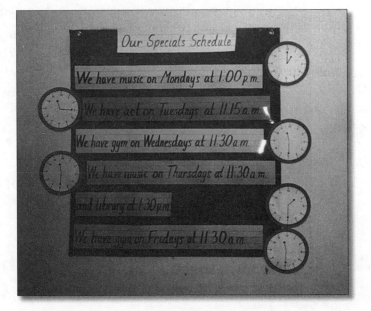

What should I know?

In addition to setting up the classroom, take a personal inventory. Be aware of expected entry and exit skills your second graders should have. Though this book lists some general goals, your school may have its own expectations. Then brush up on the skills. Break down the suggested math and language arts skills into their basic structures. Practice and be comfortable with the required operations and concepts.

What should I read?

Read as much of the second-grade literature as is possible. Children are moving into easy-reading chapter books, early chapter books, and possibly some intermediate chapter books. Be familiar with the social studies concepts and suggested reading materials. If you choose to use activities in this book that involve literature, start collecting, reading, and finding out about availability. You can be reading as the children read, but it's best to stay a couple of steps ahead of them. It's possible for an adult to read even the most complex chapter books written for this level in under an hour.

Is a plan book helpful?

Yes. First of all, plan books allow space to jot down dates, meetings, special assemblies, class lists, and a variety of other notes. Besides using it for schedules, you can think of your plan book as a kind of journal in which to write notes to yourself. Plan books kept and saved year after year serve as reminders of activities and projects, time needed for various activities, and books used for various lessons. The kind of plan book that simply has lines for each day of the week rather than little squares allows more freedom and space for recording ideas and integrated activities.

What kinds of supplies are needed in the classroom?

Teaching any grade level requires "the right stuff," so to speak. The way a classroom is stocked will depend upon available resources and funds. Whether you're starting from scratch or embellishing what's already there, consider the checklists that follow.

What might I ask students to bring to school?

By the first day of August many stores begin their back-to-school advertising campaigns. Yes, the summer is only half over, but already the general public with school-age children is being bombarded, and so are teachers. It is generally acceptable to ask students to bring certain supplies with them. Just what is allowed and what is required varies from state to state and district to district. At least one state prohibits requesting students to bring in school supplies. It's also important to consider socioeconomic situations. But whatever school supplies you ask children to bring, be sure to let parents know the purpose of each. Providing a checklist is helpful. (See page 18.) "Read Your Way Across the U.S.A.," which is mentioned in item 6 of the letter, is explained on page 51 in Chapter 4.

What about homework supplies?

Frequently, I have asked children to write, color, tape, glue, and measure at home only to have them say that they don't have materials they'll need to complete the assignments. So when I send home the list asking them to bring in school supplies, I send another list for supplies to be kept at home. If socioeconomic situations require it, you can offer the option of having some parents send extra for those in need. Include extra supplies in your classroom budget, too. That way you'll have a package available for students to borrow as needed.

What are good ways to contact students?

Writing a letter to students (see below) before school starts is a great way to introduce yourself. Including a request that they bring in a snack on the first day of school can help you begin to establish a homework routine. It lets students know that a snack is their responsibility, their *homework*. Again, if socioeconomic considerations require it, you may encourage children who participate in a breakfast program to take something extra for a mid-morning snack. If you choose to write a daily letter as suggested in this book (see page 135), the one mailed before school begins is the first letter.

Dear _____,

   Second grade is the place to be! I am so glad to be there with you this year. We can begin reading, writing, and discovering second grade together on the first day of school. Please be sure to bring your school supplies with you on that day.

   Bring a healthy snack, too! Apples, grapes, peaches, nectarines, carrots, and celery all have their own juice. Popcorn, half a sandwich, and half a bagel are good, too. It's your choice, and it's your homework every day to bring a snack to school.

   We eat our snack mid-morning, before lunch. So remember a snack to keep your stomach from going grunch, grunch, grunch!

   I'll see you on September 2, 2001, at 9:00 a.m.

Resources for supplies and professional materials

School-supply and professional catalogs are helpful in finding things, getting ideas, and making learning inquiries. Here are a few companies that will send catalogs.

Scholastic, 800-Scholas

Perfection Learning Corporation, 800-831-4190

Beckley-Cardy, 800-446-1477

Carson-Dellosa, 800-321-0943

Teaching Resource Center, 800-833-3389

Curriculum Associates, 800-225-0248

Heinemann, 800-541-2086

American Academic Suppliers, 800-325-9118

Delta Education Math/Science, 800-442-5444

Insect Lore, 800-LIVEBUG

SECOND-GRADE SUPPLIES

General Supplies:

___ #2 pencils

___ a variety of colored markers including multicultural (Crayola has several styles to choose from.)

___ black and colored sets of permanent markers (Magic Marker brand is great!)

___ erasers

___ 2"x 18" Truray construction paper—two packages each of red, orange, blue, gray, brown, green, black, purple, yellow, multicultural

___ 1 ream of 12"x 18" 80 lb. white sulfite paper

___ white glue

For Language Arts:

___ literature display bookcase (so the books face out)

___ 1 or 2 chart stands (easel) (Table chart stands are good too.)

___ 6 lined, 1-inch-ruled pads of chart paper

___ 4 to 5 packages 8"x 10½" red margin essay paper

___ 34"x 42" pocket charts

___ 8 to 10 packages assorted, 100 lb. tag board sentence strips*

___ 100-sheet hard covered, wide-ruled composition books (3 to 4 per child) (You may want to ask students to bring these in.)

___ 12 dictionaries—student and adult (more is better)

___ tape player and headphones

___ books on tape

___ Scrabble

For Math:

___ tessellations

___ unifix cubes, a set of at least 1,000

___ pattern blocks

___ base ten sets

___ fraction circles

___ student clocks (Judy clocks hold up best.)

___ tangrams

___ dice

___ K'Nex connecting toys

___ Lego toy blocks or similar toys

For Science:

___ student thermometers

___ magnifying glasses

___ plastic containers and beakers of various sizes

___ measuring cups

For Social Studies:

___ wall maps of U.S.A. and world

___ globe

___ U.S.A. atlas—student and adult

___ maps of your town

For Classroom Organization:

___ student tote bins and caddy or shelving in which to hold them (if you don't use desks)

___ plastic baskets and containers in various sizes for journals, markers, manipulative materials, books on tape

*Note: You'll need these if you choose to use pocket charts and have a Poetry Place. (See page 27.)

Dear Parents:

Welcome to second grade! It is a dynamic year of growth and mini-miracles. It is a year filled with fun and adventure. You can help, by supplying your child with the following items on the first day of school.

1. Three 100-sheet, wide-ruled, marbled composition books. Different colored covers are preferred, as this is a strategy for organization. Red or purple, green, and blue are available at Staples and Family Discount stores.
   These will be used for a reading-response journal, and a poetry journal.
   The journals will be labeled at school.

2. 1 box of 24- or 48- or 64-count Crayola crayons. (*Optional: a plastic box to hold crayons.)
   These will be used for reading, writing, math, science, and social studies activities.

3. 1 box of 24- or 36-count colored pencils (*Optional: a plastic zipper case or self-sealing plastic bag)
   These will be used for reading, writing, math, science, and social studies activities.

4. 10 sharpened #2 pencils (plain yellow are greatly preferred) (*Optional: a plastic zippered pencil case)
   These are for writing, writing, and more writing across the curriculum.

5. Three 2-pocket folders (solid colors are preferred)
   These will be used to hold homework, writing, and miscellaneous papers.

6. 1 package of 50 4" x 6" lined white index cards
   These are for keeping track of home reading. (See "Read Your Way Across the U.S.A.," attached.)

When you are shopping for these supplies to send in to school, you may wish to buy crayons, pencils, scissors, a ruler, a lined writing tablet, and a dictionary to keep at home. That way your second grader will be equipped to do his or her homework.

Please feel free to contact me if you have any questions or concerns about this list. Extra materials are always appreciated and can be put to good use. Thank you for your support. I look forward to meeting with you this year.

Sincerely,

Valerie SchifferDanoff

CHAPTER 3

Classroom Setup

The way a classroom is set up has a great impact on how you and the children function. You want to be sure your students can easily find and reach the materials they'll need to use. Consider the following questions as you plan your classroom setup.

What may a typical day in second grade look like?

The day begins with the children entering the room, checking themselves in, and signing up for lunch. They put their homework folders on their table, chat a little, then join the teacher in front of the daily letter. After exchanging some greetings, the children read and do the activities in the daily letter. This may take anywhere from 20 to 40 minutes.

Next comes reading or Reading Workshop. This begins with a discussion of books to be read and responses posted on a chart. During reading time children read, meet with the teacher, and write a response—not necessarily in that order. They may also write in their poetry journal, or their writing journal or continue independent reading. From time to time they may be reading and writing related projects at the Imagination Station. They can listen to books on tape and play word games such as Scrabble quietly.

This language arts block, including the daily letter, takes approximately 90 minutes. Then there's a snack break during which a book can be read aloud. Following that is a math lesson and math activity until lunchtime. Following lunch and recess with a read aloud is a good way to settle children for the afternoon's activities. Next comes music, gym, art, library, or computers. Then there's writing workshop, social studies, or science. Twenty to twenty-five minutes before the end of the day, homework is checked and that evening's homework assigned.

Our Specials Schedule

On Mondays we have gym at 10:50 a.m.

On Tuesdays we have music at 1:30 p.m.

On Wednesdays we have art at 11:00 a.m. and gym at 1:30 p.m.

On Thursdays we have library at 11:20 a.m.

On Fridays we have music at 2:15 p.m.

DAILY SCHEDULE			
Morning		**Afternoon**	
9:10–9:40	Daily letter	12:00–1:00	Lunch
9:40–10:50	Reading workshop	1:00–1:25	Chapter book
10:50–11:10	Story and snack	1:30–2:00	Special (teacher prep)
11:10–11:15	Cleanup	2:00–2:30	Writing, social studies
11:15–12:00	Math	2:30–2:55	Homework

How can I organize my classroom to meet the needs of second graders?

Organization and access to supplies is important. Second graders need an environment in which they can move comfortably without bumping into one another and for which they can be somewhat responsible. For example, a color-coded journal system makes it easy for children to take responsibility for their own work. Here's how: Provide storage bins of different colors—one for each kind of journal. Then color-code the journals. Even if you can't have different colored journals, the children can color over the white space on the front with a crayon. For instance, use a red bin for the poetry journal and have children lightly color the white label section on the front with a red crayon. Then have the children write their name and the name of the journal on the label—and on a color-coded label on the side. (See Reading page 41, Writing page 53, and Poetry, page 29 for more information on journals.)

What are some ways to teach responsibility?

When materials are well organized, second graders can clean up and store personal and shared items easily. If you don't use individual desks, student tote bins are almost a must. Keep shared art supplies in a common space, and make students responsible for caring for these supplies as well as their own. (See "Imagination Station" on page 30.)

How can interdependence be established?

Interdependence is a social studies concept that you can teach through your classroom management. It's important to help children realize how they are working together to create their classroom space. For example, you can design a bulletin board for which the final outcome relies on everyone's project being posted. You can also make sure to have spaces available that allow for peer coaching and cooperative groupings.

What about learning centers?

Second graders enjoy working and learning independently in learning centers, classroom areas set up with needed material. Some centers are always available and change as necessary. Others are set up to coordinate with a particular unit or subject being taught—science experiments, for example.

First graders aren't able to sustain a 60- to 90-minute reading and writing time, but second graders can. It's best to have the class reading and writing at the same time, and centers complementing these activities can be scheduled for a certain time of day or during certain times of the week as well as for particular purposes. That way the teacher is available to work with the children in the centers.

What about self-perpetuating spaces?

Self-perpetuating spaces, for which the purpose and general framework stay the same but the content changes according to curriculum and themes, empower students and give you more time to prepare and teach. A self-perpetuating classroom also provides for lots of displays of student, rather than teacher, work

What are some suggestions for spaces or bulletin boards that are self-perpetuating?

Here are some ideas I've used in my classroom.

What's Up?

Placing the words "What's Up?" on a bulletin board provides a space that can change to display any project or activity on which the class is currently working. You can start the year with it blank and progressively fill it with a variety of activities.

My Space in Our Place

MATERIALS

- tag quality sentence strips (about 10 per child)
- permanent black markers
- pencils
- children's writing journals
- pocket charts

Pocket charts are a versatile way to easily display a variety of ideas and activities. They fill a bulletin board neatly, come in a variety of sizes and colors, can be changed easily, and are nearly indestructible.

This pocket chart activity integrates math and social studies. It gives the children a chance to profile themselves and gives the class opportunities to conduct and record class surveys.

Start off the year by creating two pocket charts—one about yourself and one describing the class. The one describing the class changes as children in the class conduct surveys. Display these during the first few weeks of school. (Creating pocket-chart displays for a hallway bulletin board is a great way to introduce yourself and the members of your class to the school.)

Here are some lessons for using and changing the display. Do them in order.

LESSON 1   TEACHING LIST WRITING

1 Show the children the two charts. Together, read and discuss the content. Go over the highlights about the teacher.

2 Explain that the children will each have a chance to display their profiles (My Space), as you did, and to conduct a class survey (Our Place).

3 Have the children set up three pages in their writing journals. Title one page "Things I can tell about myself." Leave the facing page blank. Title another page "Things I would like to know about our class." Model the page setup on chart paper.

4 Explain to the children that they are going to write two lists of ten ideas or subjects for each chart. Remind them of the subjects you told about yourself and the class. Write down a couple of the ideas on the chart paper. Explain that lists are not usually sentences but short phrases of one or two words. The first list might include pets, favorite food, favorite ice cream, birthday, and so forth. The second list could have similar ideas that the whole class could be surveyed on—favorite candy, favorite color, and so on.

Ⓗ Make the list writing a homework assignment.

LESSON 2   SHARING IDEAS FROM "THINGS I CAN TELL ABOUT MYSELF."

1 Have the children prepared with pencils and their writing journals.

2 Ask them if they have ever played "Go Fish." Remind them that one person starts by saying, "Do you have...?" Tell them they'll be fishing for more ideas for their charts. This makes the activity into a game that children love. You can use the same technique for lots of other learning situations.

3 To pair children, count them off from one to whatever number is half the number of children in your class. Then number the other half by counting to that number again. Have the partners start by going over their lists and exchanging ideas and adding ideas to their lists. For instance:

> **Child 1:** Did you write favorite sport?
>
> **Child 2:** Yes. Did you write favorite dinosaur?
>
> **Child 1:** No. I'll add that to my list. Did you write brothers or sisters?
>
> **Child 2:** No. I'll add that to my list.

Once children have worked with this partner, they can go on to another partner. In a matter of a fun-filled half hour children's lists usually grow from 10 to 30 ideas.

(H) For homework, have the children choose ten ideas from their total list to write ten sentences about themselves on the blank page opposite the "Things I can tell about myself" page in their journals.

4 Before the next lesson, check the final lists for correct spelling and sentence structure.

LESSON 3   WRITING ON SENTENCE STRIPS

This activity is a great way to teach the whole class how to use the permanent markers and sentence strips.

1 Demonstrate how to write on the sentence strip with pencil and then go over the pencil with permanent marker. This saves on waste since children make mistakes and sentence strips are not cheap.

2 Discuss spacing and possible smearing. Most sentence strips have a wider part that is best used for the bottom to allow for letters such as *y* and *g*.

3 Hand out sentence strips and watch the children enjoy using something that is usually used only by their teachers. Be sure to insist that they write all their strips in pencil and check with you before they finish them with the marker.

4 Paper-clip each student's sentence strips together with a small piece of paper clipped on to indicate the order.

LESSON 4   SURVEYING

1 Tell the children that now that they have their profiles ready, the class needs to decide who will be first to put his or her sentences in the pocket chart. Some ideas may be A–Z order by first name, A–Z order by last name, birthday, lottery, and so on.

2 List the ideas and teach, show, and model how to transfer them to the survey form on page 36.

3 Conduct the survey and go over the results.

4 Teach the children how to transfer survey results to sentence strips for the chart display.

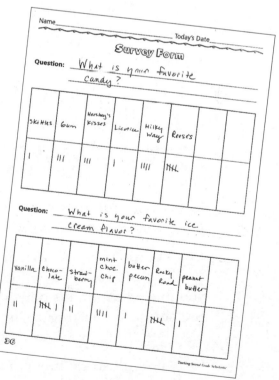

Name_____

Today's Date_____

Survey Form

Question: What is your favorite candy?

Skittles	Gum	Hershey's Kisses	Licorice	Milky Way	Reeses		
I	III	III	I	IIII	ⵜHL		

Question: What is your favorite ice cream flavor?

Vanilla	Chocolate	Strawberry	mint choc. Chip	butter pecan	Rocky Road	peanut butter	
II	ⵜHL I	II	IIII	I	ⵜHL	I	

36

Read All About It!

MATERIALS

⊙ black or colored construction paper

⊙ blank copies of the Read All About It! form (see page 35) for rough drafts and finished copy. (It includes title, by line, lines for the children to write on, and space for them to draw.)

This bulletin board displays children's writing about a book they enjoyed and, with a display of those books nearby, encourages other students to read them. The form provides a space for a short synopsis, an opinion, and an illustration.

(H) For homework, have each child bring in a book he or she recently read and enjoyed and would recommend to a friend.

LESSON 5   WRITING BOOK REVIEWS

1 Read a book with the children. Discuss what they really liked about the story. Bring out its key points or characters.

2 With the children, write on chart paper a short synopsis of the book.

3 Give each child a copy of the form for a rough draft of a Read All About It! for their chosen book. Ask them to write about what made the book interesting to them with the aim of persuading their friends to read it. This is an early model for a piece of persuasive writing.

4 Correct the rough drafts for spelling and so on. Whether or not you make other edits depends on the children's writing ability.

Read All About It!
by Mrs. Danoff

My favorite alphabet story is "Alligator Arrived with Apples," by Crescent Dragonwagon. It has animals bringing foods for every letter. I like reading about all the different animals. The pictures are colorful and funny. At the end all the animals come together for a big feast.

5 To create final copies, have the children copy their rough drafts on another form and illustrate them in the space provided.

6 Have the children share their writing. The class can vote on which book they'd like to read most. Finally, you might want to back the reviews with black construction paper and hang them on the bulletin board.

Try to have the children complete one Read All About It! each month. Hang one on top of the other so that gradually each child has a collection of his or her writing on display.

READ ALL ABOUT IT!

My favorite book from second grade is My Father's Dragon by Ruth Gannet. In the beginning Elmer meets a cat. The cat tells Elmer a story about a dragon. Elmer felt sorry for the dragon. Then Elmer got into a ship and hid in a sack that said Cranberry. When the ship stops Elmer gets on the island. Then Elmer sleeps under a tangerine tree. Then Elmer wakes up and crosses some rocks. It took him seven hours. When he got to the island he met a lot of animals. When he crosses a river he finds the dragon. Then he got out his jacknife and ripped the rope off the dragon but he did not get to cut it all because the animals were coming. Then soon the dragon and Elmer flew away. This book was the best because it was a wonderful story.

Assessment Tip

Over the months, assess each child's development of language mechanics and growth in difficulty of books read. At the end of the year, have the children each write a Read All About It! about their favorite book from second grade. Keep and display them for the first few weeks of the next school year. They'll serve as models for incoming second graders.

Poetry Place

MATERIALS

- composition books for poetry journals
- tag quality sentence strips
- pocket charts
- construction paper
- permanent markers, markers, pencils, and scissors

Poetry Place is more than a bulletin board. It's an event. Children love working in cooperative groups to choose poems, copy them onto sentence strips, and illustrate and perform them. Each child keeps a poetry journal. In these they copy the poems on display as well as other poems they find that they love. The poetry journal is also a place for children to write their own poems. Display four to five Poetry Place poems at a time and change them about every six to eight school days, depending on your schedule.

If you don't have space for four pocket charts, layer one chart on top of another, periodically shifting the one on top.

VARIATION: Have the children copy the poems onto chart paper, and glue on the illustrations. Clothespin the chart paper onto a line or stick it on a wall.

Whether you or the children choose the poems, it's important to remember to look for poems that have ten lines or less if you're using a pocket chart. Twelve lines are possible if you pin one line above and one below the pocket chart. Choose or help the children choose simple poems with few interpretive words or images.

LESSON 1 ACTING OUT POEMS

1 Gather the children in front of the display of poems. Read each poem with them and discuss each, asking them what actions they might set to the words.

2 Have the children take turns acting out the phrases in the poems.

3 Divide the class into cooperative groups, explaining that each group will act out one poem. (They'll need two 10-minute preparation sessions.) While the groups meet, circulate from group to group, offering suggestions and encouragement.

4 Have children meet in their Poetry Place groups again to rehearse their performances. Then give each group time to act out their poems for the rest of the class.

Because it's always true that some cooperative groupings work better than others, change the groups each time the poems in Poetry Place change.

LESSON 2   WRITING IN POETRY JOURNALS

The poetry journal is a place to copy and write poems and is another reading/writing activity for independent work time. A listing of excellent poetry books is on page 33.

1 Explain to the children that this is a special journal in which they can copy and illustrate poems as well as write their own.

2 Have children copy into their journals the poem they're working on with their group. Point out that each line of the poem needs its own line in their journal. Let them know that when they have time for independent work, they can copy and illustrate the other poems in their journals as well. Be sure to tell them that you expect neat handwriting.

LESSON 3   CHANGING POETRY PLACE

The first time Poetry Place changes it's more efficient to provide four or five poems from which the groups can choose rather than have the children look through books.

1 Divide the class into cooperative groups of four or five children.

2 Hand out copies of four or five poems that have been typed onto one page. Have each group choose a poem from this page.

3 Instruct children to work within their groups to divide up the lines of their poem. After each child has chosen a line, tell them to copy the line onto a sentence strip. Be sure the children write the lines in pencil first and then double-check each line to be sure the copy is correct before using the marker to go over each line. (Check page 24 for detailed instruction on using sentence strips.)

4 Once the lines are copied onto sentence strips, give children 4"x 6" pieces of paper on which to illustrate something about the poem. Then place the sentence strips in the chart and cut out the illustrations and place them near the poem.

Spelling Bee Picks

Children frequently ask, "How do you spell...?" Certain words come up over and over again. Having a space to post these words as children ask about them can save time and help establish the children's independence. Post these words on sentence strips, write them on chart paper, or place them in a pocket chart. (See page 40 for some bees and flowers you can use to decorate the space.)

Spelling 'Bees' Words of the Week

This is the place to post the spelling words each week. If you use a spelling program with a weekly word list write them permanently in A–Z order on a pad of chart paper—beginning each letter on its own page—for quick and ready reference. (See Chapter 6 for details on spelling.)

Math Space

Math Space is a great place to display of all kinds of graphs reflecting current study. For instance, if you're studying pizza (see page 157, food integration), take a survey on favorite toppings. Then teach the children to transfer survey results onto a bar graph. You might include a pocket chart that holds class surveys or graphs. A birthday graph is a great one to start off the school year. Leaving it up all year is a good way to keep track of class birthdays. (See page 36 for a blank bar graph form and survey questionnaire form that you can use to perpetuate this space.)

Imagination Station

This is basically a space in the classroom to store readily available art supplies and directions that help the children complete independent projects. Examples of projects are found throughout this book.

Suggested supplies: markers, writing paper, envelopes, colored pencils, scissors, glue, T squares, rulers, construction paper, crayons. Placing these supplies in appropriately sized baskets, as pictured, can keep this space neat and organized for easy use and cleanup.

Here's a great first project that can help teacher and class get to know each other better.

LESSON 1   CLOTHES LINES

MATERIALS

- © various colors of construction paper
- © composition paper
- © string (Thin cord can be purchased for about 5¢ a foot at a hardware store.)
- © sentence strips (on which you write the directions)
- © one copy per child of "My Clothes Lines" Questionnaire (You can photocopy the sample included at the end of this chapter.)
- © one set of clothes (made from the patterns on pages 38–39) per child
- © glue, scissors, crayons, markers

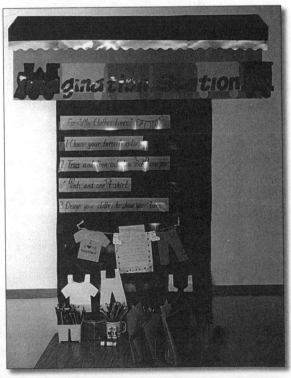

I read *The Bag I am Taking to Grandma's House* by Shirley Neitzel (Scholastic, 1995) and *Clothesline* by Jez Alborough (Walker Books, 1993) when starting this project. Make a model clothes line as shown in the photo.

1 Discuss how we personalize our clothes—colors we choose to wear, logos on our T-shirts, favorite sports, and so on.

2 Share your model clothes line and go over directions for filling in the questionnaire. Explain that "clothes line" is a play on words. Tell the children that they will write "lines"

about themselves on the clothes patterns as you did to learn a little about each other and then hang them on a clothes line. First, everyone needs to make a clothes line.

(H) 3 Send the questionnaires home as homework or have the children fill them out in class.

4 Once the children have completed their questionnaires, have them rewrite the sentences into a paragraph about themselves, on composition paper. This is a good opportunity to discuss paragraph writing, explaining that a paragraph is group of sentences about one subject.

5 Give the children their sets of clothes patterns and let them decorate these.

6 The children can also decorate their paragraph papers around the margins. Then have them cut tabs at the

margins of the papers and wrap these and the tabs on the paper clothes around a clothes line cord and glue them down. Or look for mini-clothespins, which are available in craft stores.

Classroom Charts

Classroom charts contain information that the children will need to refer to again and again— lists of homonyms; words with special attributes, which are word detective lists (see page 77 in the spelling chapter); reading response ideas; independent activities; and much more. You can make these available in several ways: on a flip chart placed at child level, on bulletin boards, or typed up and kept in a class reference book (a three-ring binder).

What are some ideas for setting up a class library?

It's essential to set up a classroom space for literature, reference books, dictionaries, books on tape, poetry books, class published books, and so on. A book rack; a tape recorder with headphones; a small, round table and chairs; and some large pillows are some amenities that can make the library inviting. Start subscribing to book clubs through which publishers give extra books and bonus points that you can use to start or increase your book collection. (Scholastic at 800-Scholas is a good place to start.) Remember that children enjoy having multiple copies of the same book to share and read together. Enhance the curriculum by choosing books for the library that are appropriate for the subject at hand. Beginning the school year with books about school is one possibility. A list of great books is found below.

Now the classroom is a prepared environment. Read on to learn more about reading, writing, and arithmetic—and more.

Good poetry books for second graders

Bing Bang Boing by Douglas Florian. Harcourt, Brace & Co., 1994.

A Pizza the Size of the Sun by Jack Prelutsky. Greenwillow Books, 1996.

Falling Up by Shel Silverstein. HarperCollins, 1996.

Kids Pick the Funniest Poems selected by Bruce Lansky. Simon & Schuster, 1991.

Animals Animals selected by Eric Carle. The Putnam Publishing Group, 1989.

The Sweet and Sour Animal Book by Langston Hughes. Oxford University Press, 1994.

Did You See What I Saw? by Kay Winters. Penguin, 1996.

What's on the Menu? selected by Bobbye S. Goldstein. Puffin, 1995.

Echoes for the Eye by Barbara Juster Esbensen. HarperCollins, 1996.

The Wild Bunch by Dee Lillegard. G.P. Putnam & Sons, 1997.

Poetry Place Anthology. Scholastic, 1990.

You Be Good and I'll be Night by Eve Merriam. William Morrow & Co., 1996.

The Random House Book of Poetry selected by Jack Prelutsky. Random House, 1983.

Read Aloud Rhymes for the Very Young selected by Jack Prelutsky. Alfred A. Knopf, 1986.

Good books about school for second graders

Miss Nelson Is Back by Henry Allard. Houghton Mifflin & Co., 1982.

Miss Nelson Has a Field Day by Henry Allard. Houghton Mifflin & Co., 1985.

Miss Nelson Is Missing by Harry Allard. Houghton Mifflin, 1982.

My Worst Days Diary by Suzanne Altman. Bantam Books, 1995.

This Is the Way We Go to School by Edith Baer. Scholastic, 1990.

The One in the Middle is the Green Kangaroo by Judy Blume. Bantam Doubleday, 1981.

The Principal's New Clothes by Stephanie Calmenson. Scholastic, 1991.

The Best Teacher in the World by Bernice Chardiet and Grace Maccarone. Scholastic, 1990.

Second-Grade Friends by Miriam Cohen. Scholastic, 1993.

Where Does the Teacher Live? by Paula Kurzband Feder. Penguin, 1979.

Miss Malarkey Doesn't Live in Room 10 by Judy Finchler. Walker and Co., 1995.

Today Was a Terrible Day by Patricia Reilly Giff. Penguin, 1984.

Chrysanthemum by Kevin Henkes. Greenwillow, 1991.

Coaching Ms. Parker by Carla Heymsfeld. Aladdin, 1992.

The Day the Teacher Went Bananas by James Howe. E.P. Dutton, 1984.

Ride Your Elephant to School by Doug Johnson. Scholastic, 1995.

The First Day of School by Tony Johnston. Scholastic, 1997.

The Teacher from Outer Space by Justine Korman. Troll, 1994.

Drop Everything , It's D.E.A.R. Time! by Ann McGovern. Scholastic, 1993.

The Show-and-Tell Frog by Joanne Oppenheim. Bantam, 1992.

I Was a Second Grade Werewolf by Daniel Pinkwater. E.P. Dutton, 1983.

Mrs. Toggle and the Dinosaur by Robin Pulver. Scholastic, 1991.

Ruby the Copycat by Peggy Rathmann. Scholastic, 1991.

The Flying School Bus by Seymour Reit. Western Publishing, 1990.

Cream of Creature from the School Cafeteria by Mike Thaler. Avon Books, 1989.

A Hippopotamus Ate the Teacher by Mike Thaler. Avon Books, 1981.

The Teacher from the Black Lagoon by Mike Thaler. Scholastic, 1989.

The Toll-Bridge Troll by Patricia Rae Wolff. Harcourt Brace & Co., 1995.

Series books

The Kids of the Polk Street School by Patricia Reilly Giff. Bantam Doubleday, 1984.

Pink and Rex by James Howe. Avon Books, 1991.

Horrible Harry in Room 2B by Suzy Kline. Penguin, 1989.

Read All About It!

by _____

_____

_____

_____

_____

_____

_____

_____

_____

_____

Survey Form

Question: _____

_____

Question: _____

_____

Teaching Second Grade Scholastic

Questionnaire for "My Clothes Lines"

My name is _____.

What kind of clothes do you like wearing best?

I like wearing _____ best.

What is your favorite color?

My favorite color is _____.

I also like _____.

What is your favorite season?

My favorite season is _____

because _____.

What kind of weather do you like best?

I like _____ days best.

What do you like to do when you're not in school?

When I'm not in school I like to _____

_____.

Clothes Templates

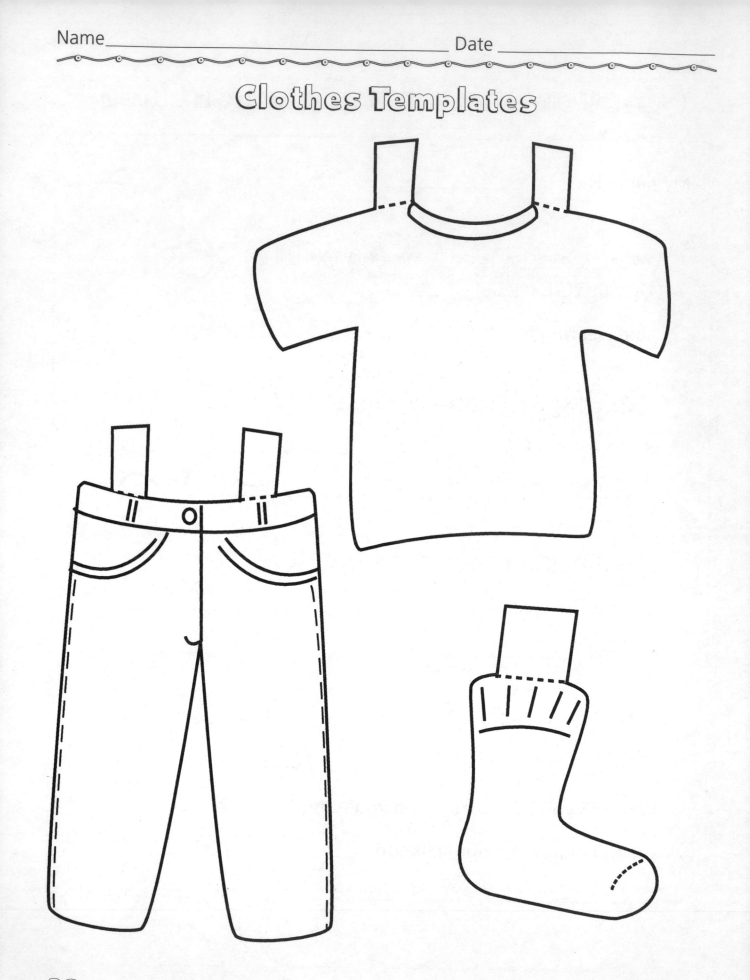

Teaching Second Grade Scholastic

Bee and Flower Templates

Reading

Second-grade readers have a great time! They love to use the abilities and skills they acquired in first grade. Even if they haven't read over the summer and are out of practice, you can quickly coax them back to their comfort zone.

Flat Stanley
Read and Respond

Chapter 1
- list other ways someone could be flattened

Chapter 2
- List things you would want to try to do if you were flat

Chapter 3
- List 5 flat things Stanley could be.

Chapter 4
- List 5 reasons why Stanley would want to stay flat.

Chapter 5
- List 5 other ways to make Stanley round again.

1   2-10-
- Reading Responses

Read - It's Valentine's Day or
     - Best Friends or
     - Arthur's Valentine

① Write ♡ Riddle A Friend ♡
♡ Write riddle in Reading Notebook. Write at least **3** clues, then 'Guess who!'
② Copy onto writing paper
③ Glue onto 12" x 18" white paper. Then fold paper.
♡ Draw clues on outside.
⑤ Draw your friend inside next to riddle.

② It's Valentine's Day - Choose a poem. Copy and illustrate.
Arthur's Valentine - List at least ⑤ ways to show someone you like him or her.
Best Friends - List at least ⑤ reasons why a friend is important to have.

What are second-grade reading skills?

Second graders can be expected to understand how to read and to apply and interpret periods, quotation marks, commas, question marks, and exclamation points. This means they can read with expression. They're learning about paragraphs, understanding subtle humor and inference, separating fact from fiction, reading more in the content areas, continuing to decode phonetically, practicing cloze, defining new vocabulary, using a table of contents and an index, understanding chapters, and continuing to work on comprehension of what they are reading. Combining skills with language-rich experiences continues the growth of the second-grade reader.

How can reading be taught in second grade?

This, of course, depends on the children in the class and the materials you've been provided. However, no matter what materials are available or how proficient the children are at reading, practice with phonics, contextual analysis, structural analysis, sight words, and vocabulary are important.

My goal in this book is not to detail how to teach reading, but to describe second-grade readers, point out some of their needs, and provide some helpful techniques. (See the resources at the end of this chapter for valuable information about various approaches to teaching reading.)

What kinds of materials are appropriate for second-grade readers?

I prefer to have a large collection of fiction and nonfiction trade literature including plays and poetry. I provide a reading response journal for each child. If you're using a basal reading program, it will determine the foundation of your reading instruction. There are ways to enhance a basal program with flexible groupings, full-class reads, text sets, and large-group shared reading.

What is needed to teach reading with trade literature?

Teaching reading with trade literature is extremely dependent upon your expertise at teaching the strategies and skills your students need to decode new vocabulary and interpret the text in a meaningful way. It's critical never to rely on just reading a book to teach reading. Children need to be taught and to practice the strategies and skills—for example: spelling, vocabulary, comprehension, cloze— they'll be tested on later. Book talks, flexible groups, and response journals can teach and reinforce the kind of growth needed to further develop second-grade readers. Ongoing assessment will help you decide what to teach and how.

What can be expected of a second-grade reader?

Second graders can be very impatient about taking the time to decode and define new vocabulary. Some feel that they're readers already; others have carried over from first grade the frustrations of learning to read. All children need to be encouraged and reminded that they're still learning to read.

Whenever you assign independent reading, have the children record new vocabulary in their response journals. Check to be sure that they've noted unfamiliar words. You'll need to identify words you want to bring to the children's attention. Present these on a chart and discuss them as part of the book talk. (See more reading response possibilities below.)

What's a good way to assess incoming second graders?

First, determine where they left off in first grade. Second, find out what kind of reading, if any, they were doing over the summer. Third, note what they choose to read during independent reading. Finally, read with each child individually to see what strategies they're using to decode new vocabulary and to define new vocabulary. Discuss the text you read with them, and ask both direct and inferential questions.

You can also use a running record throughout the year. Basically that involves using two copies of an excerpt of text. The child reads from one and, while he or she reads, the teacher notes information about word accuracy and the strategies the child is using.

From the beginning it's important to get a more general, more dynamic assessment of each child by getting to know each child. What type of learner is the child? How much can the child be challenged?

What is a good way to decide what book to start each child off with?

It is always best to start at a comfort zone. That is, encourage the child to read a book that he or she will be successful with. Even if the child says he or she has been reading more complex text over the summer, it might be best to step the level back a bit. School is different. Guided reading is different. Summer reading is different.

For example, consider a student like Mabel. Mabel says that over the summer, she's read chapter books that a strong second-grade, early third-grade reader could handle. But given similar material in class, she misses more than five words on the first page. When she brings a book from home that she and her mother say she'd read over the summer, she has difficulty reading it.

A check of Mabel's first-grade reading list reveals that at the end of last year she'd just started to read early chapter books, like *Frog and Toad* by Arnold Lobel (HarperCollins). She had not become a reader until the very end of first grade. She needs more experience with early chapter books now at the beginning of second grade. I welcome at least six children like this each year.

On the other hand, there are students like Abel. Abel has been a fluent reader since close to the beginning of first grade. Still, by the beginning of second grade he hasn't advanced beyond early chapter books. Abel also needs to be slowly coaxed and given the experience with early chapter books. Then he'll be ready to move on to higher-level chapter books such as the *Cam Jansen* series by David Adler (Penguin) and *Second-Grade Friends* by Miriam Cohen (Scholastic, 1993), and *Nate the Great* by Marjorie Weinman Sharmat (Putnam, 1982).

Other children enter second grade as very fluent readers, reading books that are inappropriate for their age. They rely heavily on their decoding fluency. They can decode words that they can't define. These children are helped by being exposed to such second-grade literature as *Horrible Harry in Room 2B* by Suzy Kline (Penguin, 1989), as well as the titles mentioned above.

Some children enter second grade not yet reading. My experience has been that these children become readers quickly. Perhaps they're more developmentally ready, and perhaps peer pressure is kicking in more strongly now. Also, peer coaching is much more available, with as much as 80 percent of the class reading and ready to help others.

Those children just beginning to read in second grade are helped immensely by having readers reading around them—and reading to and with them. They also need a comfort zone, but one that appears respectable for their grade. A book like *I Was a Second Grade Werewolf* by Daniel Pinkwater (Penguin, 1983) can be just the thing, especially since everyone wants to read it!

One last type of child to watch for is the child who may have a learning disability even though it didn't appear so in first grade. If a second grader is still struggling with recognizing letters and/or recalling or using letter sounds by the end of October, further investigation by the school's learning resource team is in order.

Whatever level or comfort zone at which your students are beginning the year, starting with alphabet stories provides a wide range of literature and reading levels. All the children in the class can succeed within this genre. Alphabet books are also perfect for assessment. (See page 144 for more on alphabet stories.)

How about phonics?

Learning and using phonics strategies are an ongoing necessity for both reading and writing. However, phonics needn't drive the program. Children who have difficulty hearing, transferring letter sounds to corresponding letters, and blending sounds are likely to struggle while they develop fluency. They may need extra practice and reinforcement with these skills as they enter second grade. Children who enter second grade with strong fluency still need practice with phonics skills, too. The list of reading responses on page 49 includes practice for phonics strategies. (The "Daily Letter" in Chapter 10 on page 135 also includes phonics reinforcement.)

Children may be reading more complex vocabulary now, and they may need to be able to use sounds to say the word and context clues to figure out what a new word means. Yet second-grade readers may be so proficient at reading that they've forgotten how to sound out a word. Additionally, they frequently don't want to take the time to find out how to say a new word or figure out what it means. It's important to require readers to decode and define new vocabulary. You'll likely need to remind, coax, and encourage them, and to demonstrate how to apply the appropriate skills. It's helpful to demonstrate how to use the dictionary as soon as possible. Second graders love the dictionary once they learn how to use it.

A holistic approach to reading immerses children in literature and literature experiences. An eclectic gathering of language-arts materials and teaching methods promotes learning. Teaching reading cannot be delegated to a certain time of the day; neither can phonics. Whenever new vocabulary appears or a learner is searching for a skill with which to better understand written language, it's best to employ whatever is needed to accomplish the goal of understanding. Lifelong readers and learners do not let a word stand in their way.

What about reading groups?

However you group your students, children love reading the same book and then sharing their excitement. You can group children for reading very traditionally by ability level or in flexible groups. When children are reading chapter books, replace small-group, guided reading with book talks focused more toward comprehension and vocabulary skills than on decoding skills. Flexible groups give children still developing fluency the opportunity to have varied experiences with books, their teacher, and their peers.

What are flexible reading groups?

You can look at flexible grouping in two ways. One is to vary the students in the groups. The same children aren't always reading together. The other is to consider different types of groupings. For example, in paired reading, two children read together. This technique can encourage a peer coaching or simply allow two children to share a book they both like. Another kind of grouping is whole class. Everyone has the same book, and the whole class can sit in a circle and read chorally or take turns going around the circle; or all the students can read independently and be ready for a full class response, written or verbal.

Flexible groupings may also be decided by interest in a particular book. The teacher may ask, "Who would like to read this book?" Or they can be determined by type of book—trade literature, fiction, nonfiction, plays, atlases, phone books, tapes, poetry, or even a basal series.

Another good way to use flexible groups (or paired reading) effectively is to have text (or web) sets—several sets of different books on the same subject. Let the children know that everyone will get a chance to read all the books in turn. That way it's only a matter of which group member will read which book first. When the children are working with sets of books on the same subject, responses can be inter-textual. That is, children can respond to the same set of questions for each of the books or respond with comparisons among the books.

It's best to have all students reading at the same time when you're using flexible groups. Hand out the books and let everyone start reading or looking through the book. (This is also known as a book walk for children who can't yet read independently.) During this time, you can read with groups of children or with individual children. With this approach nonreaders and beginning readers have the support of peer coaches around them.

In second grade it is important to help children advance beyond decoding to increase understanding and interpretive skills. Flexible reading groups that integrate fiction and nonfiction can be a key element in accomplishing this goal. Such groups instill confidence in the children you teach and support effective classroom management by allowing you the time to design and teach mini-lessons for particular needs, and by allowing the children time for extended independent reading.

How much time can children spend reading?

Second graders can spend from 20 minutes to about an hour and 15 minutes reading and working independently and with the teacher. Setting that expectation the very first time the children are reading is the best way to establish it. My

approach to having children read in flexible groups during Reading Workshop differs from SSR (sustained silent reading) or DEAR (drop everything and read) time. Besides reading independently, children are having book talks, writing responses, and reading with me. Having every child begin reading at the same time keeps the room quiet and on task.

What are some of the ways this time can be used?

The children that are reading chapter books might read for 40 minutes independently, then continue working another 15 minutes on an independent reading response they share during a book talk for another 15 minutes. The children reading a picture book with a medium amount of text might read for 15 minutes and spend 20 to 30 minutes in a book talk/mini-lesson with the teacher and then another 15 minutes writing a reading response. The children still learning to read may spend 15 to 25 minutes independently "walking through" and reading the book with the teacher, 15 minutes working independently, another 15 minutes learning and responding to the book, and still another 15 minutes of independent practice.

What should the teacher do while all the children are reading?

Having all the children reading at the same time eliminates that "waiting to read with the teacher" time You can read with one child and small groups of children as determined by individual needs. Before some children start reading, you can conduct book talks to set up a response, walk through the book, or highlight new vocabulary. While children are reading you can check for comprehension and vocabulary skills. When children have completed a book, you can encourage a response, check on vocabulary, or react to a completed response.

What can children do when they've finished reading?

It is very important for children to know what to do when they've finished reading. I highly recommend that they prepare a reading response (see page 49). Other independent classroom activities such as working on their Poetry Journal, doing an Imagination Station project listening to tapes, or writing in a personal journal keep the children reading and writing during this time. Posting a list of the possibilities is helpful.

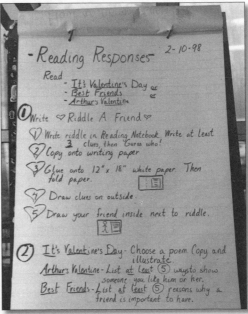

What is a reading response journal?

My students' reading response journals are black, marbled composition books in which the children keep a record of the books they've read, the date on which they finished the book, and a written response to each book. It helps me and my students keep track of the books they've read, and how they've grown in reading and writing. It's also a place for students to keep a record of new vocabulary they've learned from the book, and to work on new vocabulary and mini–reading-lesson topics like compound words, quotations, contractions, suffixes, and so on.

What are some appropriate reading responses for second graders?

The list shown on page 49 provides some of the many possible reading responses. It isn't possible to respond to every book in the same way. And it's important to tailor responses to learning growth. For example, asking a child who can not yet read to write a letter to the author wouldn't be appropriate. (You could help a child do this during a book talk.) A more appropriate response for this child would be one that develops phonics skills, such as writing down all the words that begin with a particular consonant blend (digraph) or all the words with a particular spelling pattern such as [CVCe]. Children love to become "word detectives."

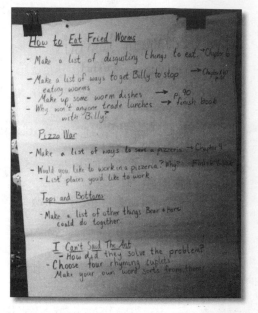

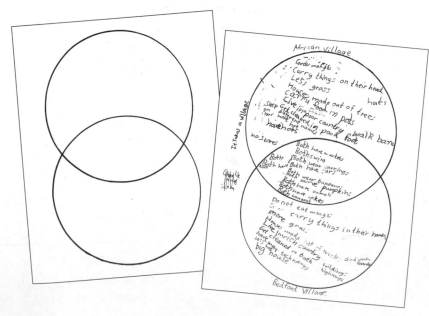

Appropriate Reading Responses for Second Graders

Have children:

- Create a KWL about a subject or character.

- Become word detectives for spelling patterns, rhymes, suffixes, new vocabulary.

- Write phonogram lists based on spelling patterns from vocabulary in the story.

- Find the place where it tells... (To check on comprehension, have the child answer verbally during a book talk.)

- Create graphic organizers: i.e., Venn diagrams, story maps, character maps.

- Choose two characters from two different books and tell what would happen if they met.

- Sequence the main events in the story.

- Answer intra-textual questions: questions about information in the story or about things inferred by connecting information in the story. (i.e., *who*, *what*, *where*, *when*, and *how* questions)

- Answer extra-textual questions by connecting information in the story to their personal knowledge or ideas.

- Answer inter-textual questions by connecting information from one story to that of another on the same theme.

- For chapter books, answer questions (which have been posted on a chart) for each chapter.

- Write chapter summaries.

- Redesign the cover of the book.

- Create a mobile of the book's setting and characters.

- Work together in groups of four to six to retell the story pictorially using triaramas.

- Work together in groups of four to six to retell the story pictorially through a mural.

- Create a "Wanted" Poster for one of the characters.

- Write a list of what they learned from a nonfiction book.

- Pretend they're meeting one of the characters and write the dialogue that takes place.

- Develop a Readers Theater.

What are some good books for the whole class to read at the same time?

There is nothing like having the whole class read the same book at the same time. Some book suggestions are listed on pge 52. If you've heard the expression "two heads are better than one," imagine 20 to 24! However, be prepared. The discussions can get very intense as everyone has a definite opinion on what is going to happen next. It can be a race for time as all search for "the place where the character..." But just one caution: full-class reads should not be overused. It is important to spread them out.

Full-class reads are an excellent way to teach in the content areas. A nonfiction full-class read can be very instructive and exciting. You can start with the KWL format and have the children search for answers to their questions as they read.

If you choose a book that one or two children have already read, chances are they don't remember every detail. As the class reads and discusses they'll discover things they hadn't noticed before. Be sure to give these students positive reinforcement with comments like:

Aren't you lucky to revisit the book with your whole class.

You and I can have some private book talks.

Great! Then I hope you can be a peer coach and read with...

What about Readers Theater or plays?

Second graders love Readers Theater and plays. Plays are just about the best way to spur on that reluctant reader. If a child needs a reading coach, a play is the perfect vehicle. Children can read from scripts and make their characters' likeness on a paper plate to be strung and worn around their necks. They love to put the plays on for other classes and grade levels.

Making a poster for the performance is a fun reading response or homework assignment. Children can also make some wonderful posters using the Kid Pix computer program by Craig Hickman (Broderbund Software, 1991). Two good resources for plays are:

Plays Around the Year. Scholastic, 1995.

Primary Reader's Theater Pack, from Curriculum Press, 800-225-0248.

What about reading chapter books to second graders?

They absolutely adore it. Second graders are ready to listen and hold on to information. They savor the continuance of a story. It is so much fun to hear the clamor as they return from lunch and be greeted with "It's Piggle-Wiggle time." That, of course, is part of the name of a highly recommended chapter book *(Mrs. Piggle-Wiggle* by Betty MacDonald. HarperCollins, 1949, 1975). *The Prince of the Pond* by Donna Jo Napoli (Penguin, 1994), *Frindle* by Andrew Clements (Simon & Schuster, 1996), and *The Lion, the Witch and the Wardrobe* by C.S. Lewis (Simon & Schuster, 1950, 1996) are others the children love to hear.

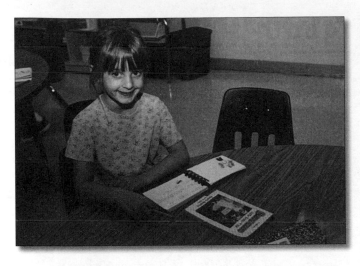

What is a good way to encourage and keep track of reading at home?

The children in my class have enjoyed an activity we call Read Your Way Across the U.S.A. I ask each child to bring in a package of 4" x 6" lined white index cards. We bind these with plastic binding. (Or you can buy them prebound.) Two more cards serve as front and back covers. I send home the following letter:

Dear Parents:

To help support your child's reading in school and at home, our class is keeping a set of 4"x 6" index cards fastened together and called

Read Your Way Across the U.S.A.

When your child completes a book at home or as extra reading in school, he or she writes down the title, author, characters, and setting on one side of the card and creates an illustration for the book on the other side.

Whenever a card is completed, your child "visits a state" and receives a state sticker on the card. I've asked the children to bring the books from their home reading to school in case they need help in "carding" the book. Our goal is to read 50 books by the last day of school.

On the front cover of the card packet there is a small map of the continental United States to help your child quickly keep track of which states he or she has visited. This process integrates with the New York State Social Studies curriculum for Grade 2.

The children have already "read their way" to one state and are very excited about their travel. They consult the map to figure out where they want to go next. Each child chooses his or her own direction.

Books can take you places.

Thanks for your support.

Sincerely,
Valerie SchifferDanoff

Once the children complete books at home, they bring them to school and complete the information mentioned in the letter. For nonfiction or poetry books children simply record them as such.

The idea is for each card to resemble a postcard. Once the card is complete, it is checked by the teacher, and the child receives a state stamp sticker (available at educational stores or from catalogs). The goal is for each child to have read 50 books in addition to their reading workshop books. A book of 80 pages or more can take up two cards or even three if it's longer than 150 pages. The child can simply write the name of the book on the second and third cards or add more pictures.

Reading in second grade is growing into knowing. Children learn the special joy of becoming lifelong readers. They discover the richness their literacy can provide.

Resources for teaching reading

Fountas, Irene C. and Gay Su Pinnell. *Guided Reading*. Heinemann, 1996.

Johnson, T. and Louis, D. *Literacy Through Literature*. Heinemann, 1987.

Routman, Regie. *Transitions from Literature to Literacy*. Heinemann, 1988.

SchifferDanoff, Valerie. *The Scholastic Integrated Language Arts Resource Book*. Scholastic, 1995.

Good books to try as full-class reads

Everybody Cooks Rice by Norah Dooley. Carolrhoda, 1991.

It's Thanksgiving by Jack Prelutsky. Greenwillow, 1982.

It's Valentine's Day by Jack Prelutsky. William Morrow & Co., 1983.

It Takes a Village by Jane Cowen-Fletcher. Scholastic, 1994.

Flat Stanley by Jeff Brown. Harper Trophy, 1964, 1992.

The Seven Treasure Hunts by Betsy Byars. Harper Trophy, 1998.

My Father's Dragon by Ruth Stiles Gannet. Random House, 1948.

Great reads for second graders

The Stories Julian Tells by Ann Cameron. Random House, 1991.

The Adam Joshua Capers by Janice Lee Smith. Harper Trophy, 1984.

The Adventures of Ali Baba Bernstein by Johanna Hurwitz. William Morrow, 1995.

Adventures of the Shark Lady by Ann McGovern. Scholastic, 1998.

Amber Brown Wants Extra Credit by Paula Danzinger. The Putnam Grosset Group, 1996.

Beanie (Not Beanhead) and the Magic Crystal, by Susan Wojciechowski. Candlewick, 1997.

Bunnicula by James Howe. Scholastic, 1984.

Busybody Nora by Johanna Hurwitz. Penguin, 1991.

Cam Jansen (series) by David A. Adler. Penguin, 1981.

A Case for Jennie Archer by Ellen Conford. Little, Brown, 1988.

Catwings, Catwings Returns, and *Wonderful Alexander and the Catwings* by Ursula K. LeGuin. Orchard Books, 1994.

A Dragon in the Family by Jackie French Koller. Little, Brown, 1993.

Ghost at Dougal Castle by Laura Jean Allen. Harper Trophy, 1994.

Gila Monsters Meet You at the Airport by Marjorman Weinman Sharmat. Simon & Schuster, 1980.

Go West, Swamp Monster by Mary Blount Christian. Penguin, 1985.

Godzilla Ate My Homework by Marcia Thornton Jones. Scholastic, 1997.

Horrible Harry in Room 2B by Suzy Kline. Penguin.

How to Eat Fried Worms by Thomas Rickwell. Yearling Dell, 1973.

I'm Dracula, Who Are You, by Mike Thaler. Troll Communications, 1996.

Jenius the Amazing Guinea Pig by Dick King Smith. Hyperion, 1996.

The Littles by John Peterson. Scholastic, 1967.

The Magic Goose by Daniel Pinkwater. Scholastic, 1997.

Max Malone Makes a Million by Charlotte Herman. Henry Holt, 1991.

Midnight Magic by Amy Gordon. Bridgewater Books, 1995.

Mystery in the Night Woods by John Peterson. Scholastic, 1969.

Nasty Stink Sneaker by Eve Bunting. HarperCollins, 1994.

Nate the Great (series) by Marjorie Weinman Sharmat. The Putnam Publishing Group, 1982.

The Puppy Sister by S.E. Hinton. Delacorte, 1995.

Rollow and Tweedy by Laura Jean Allen. Harper Trophy, 1994.

Ronald Morgan Goes to Bat by Patricia Reilly Giff. Penguin, 1990.

Scrambled Eggs and Spider Legs by Gary Hogg. Scholastic, 1998.

Second Grade Ape by Daniel Pinkwater. Scholastic, 1998.

Something Queer in the Wild West by Elizabeth Levy. Hyperion, 1997.

The Spray-Paint Mystery by Angela Shelf Medearis. Scholastic, 1969.

The Stinky Sneakers Contest by Julie Anne Peters. Little, Brown and Co., 1992.

CHAPTER 5

Writing

The best thing about writing with second graders is that they like it. Actually, they love it. When it's time to stop writing instead of hearing the sigh of relief and the scurry to put away papers heard in first grade, you hear, "Do we have to?" Yet, when the year begins, second graders have no idea what they are capable of writing. Writing workshops and mini-lessons are very important. Modeling is essential. Time to explore and reflect upon good literary examples contributes to success. In second grade, writing is everywhere, as is reading, because now children have acquired the skills and are developmentally ready to use them.

What are second-grade writing skills?

Second graders are learning about and practicing:

- sentence structure
- punctuation
- quotation marks
- dialogue
- paragraphing
- correct spelling
- descriptive writing
- expressive writing

What is Writing Workshop?

Writing Workshop is basically a time set aside during which children write. Like anything else in the classroom, it should be established with precedents and expectations. Writing Workshop can begin with a lesson or mini-lesson that targets a particular skill; a literary example and discussion; a lesson introducing or reinforcing a genre of writing and then continuing with 30 to 45 minutes of writing without any interruptions.

While children are writing, you can conference with individual writers or work with a small group of writers. The writing process includes a rough draft, teacher and peer conferences, editing, rewrites, and final copy. It can be helpful to have a computer available and to teach children how to write directly on the computer. (See the references on page 68 for excellent books about teaching writing.)

How is Writing Workshop introduced?

Good literature can serve as a model for teaching children how to write a whole story, with a beginning, middle, and end. Second graders are learning how to incorporate more descriptive detail and extend their use of vocabulary. Explaining that they can also be authors places a great deal of respect in their hands—along with their pencil.

Read *The Art Lesson* by Tomie dePaola (G.P. Putnam, 1989), and share some of his other books. Discuss how Tomie is now a writer. Or read *Arthur Writes a Story* by Marc Brown (Little Brown, 1996). Or try *What Do Authors Do?* by Eileen Christelow (Houghton Mifflin, 1995) and one of her other books, *The Great Pig Escape* (Houghton Mifflin, 1994), for example.

What are some suggestions for Writing Workshop mini-lessons?

The best way to decide on an appropriate mini-lesson is to assess the class to determine what children are ready for or what they need. Be the judge of when to give a particular lesson and to whom it should be given. A suggested list is found on page 55. Whether it's the whole class or a small group of children, remember to use your students' writing to model and teach. Let the child whose work is being shared know that his or her work is serving as a model to help teach everyone else. But before you begin, be sure to ask the children permission to use their writing, and make sure they understand how much you value their work even though some changes may be suggested.

Looking At A Tree
I have a tree that gives my mom's garden shade.
It has a bird house.
It gives two chairs shade too.
It give my dirt pile shade too.
It is taller than my house.

The tree gives two chair shade too.
This tree is taller than my house.

There is a bird house in this tree.

When I look at my tree I see squirrels.

There are red leaves in the tree.

My tree is an apple tree.
This tree is a tree that changes color later.
In a hole there are mushrooms.
There are wind chimes hanging from it.
And my dad put stocky stuff around it.
The bark is gray. The tree is in my backyard.

color, size, shape

GOOD WRITING LESSONS AND MINI-LESSONS FOR SECOND GRADERS

Sentences	Character mapping	Punctuation
Adjectives	Descriptive language	Spelling
Cause and effect	Expressive language	List writing
Problem and problem solving	Diagramming: using a pictorial representation within text	Observations
Story mapping		KWL chart
Structural analysis for beginning/middle/end	Poetry	Research
	Paragraphing	Word maps

Does spelling count?

Second graders are transitioning from temporary spelling to correct spelling. In first grade children may have used "inventive" spelling, but second graders are very aware that there is a correct way to spell. A Writing Workshop mini-lesson can be a spelling lesson—particularly if the children are writing about a specific subject. Brainstorming vocabulary words on a chart gets second graders thinking and provides a list of correctly spelled words. Encouraging correct spelling without discouraging the flow of writing is a balance well worth the effort and patience it takes. (See Chapter 6 for more on spelling.)

How about handwriting?

By kindergarten, children have developed a grip. Good or bad, it's probably the one they've got for life. Typical handwriting problems are: too much pencil pressure, which can cause smearing; too little pencil pressure; spacing too close or too far; letters that are formed incorrectly.

Modeling penmanship and providing practice is part of teaching writing. It's important to remind children that if they write something wonderful, they want other people to be able to read it. How strict the teacher is about penmanship is up to the individual.

Many school districts have handwriting programs. My district uses the D'Nealian program, for which the letters are formed on a slant and have little tails. This technique is designed to lead to cursive writing, which is taught in third grade. Some districts teach cursive as early as first grade.

(H) Giving practice sheets for handwriting is a good homework exercise.

What kinds of writing are second graders capable of doing?

Second graders are ready to write in various genres. They can keep a personal journal. They can write their own creative stories. They can incorporate cause and effect. They can learn how to research a subject and do inquiry-based writing. They can write poetry. Truly, given the right mini-lessons and modeling, second graders are ready to write just about anything. I like to begin on the very first day with journal writing.

What is journal writing?

For journal writing, each child writes personal thoughts and feelings in some sort of composition book. A second grader can usually fill a hard cover composition book of 100 pages by the end of the year. Some teachers write back to the children in their journals. I recommend having the journals include only the children's writing. This gives them permission to write how they feel, what they want—and most important to know that no judgment or assessment is marring their writing. This setup doesn't mean the teacher can't make comments or corrections. Stick-on notes work well for this purpose.

What can children write about in their journals?

You can ask children to write about specific subjects in their journals as long as they include their own thoughts, reactions, and so on. For example, you might have the children write about their experiences, science observations, or their understanding of a math concept. On Mondays children love to tell about their weekend. You might ask the children to write just that in their journals every Monday. A colleague of mine suggests that children write a "Nothing Letter" to their parents every Friday and then take their journals home to share. This way parents can read about what their child has done in school that week as well as any other entries.

 You can also send journals home during the week with specific requests for personal responses. You'll see some of these requests throughout the book. (For example, see "A Squirrel Observation," page 127.)

What is a good way to teach journal writing?

Like anything else, the best way to teach writing is by modeling. Show the children how you would write in your own journal—to yourself or to someone else. Explain that keeping a journal helps the writer to record and remember thoughts that he or she might have forgotten later. Right from the first day of school, I tell the children that the letter I post each day is a journal I'm writing to them. I use the letter to start mini-lessons. (See Chapter 10 on daily letters for more information.) Suggestions for other mini-lessons are found on page 58.

When and how should I have my students begin journal writing?

You can introduce journal writing on the first day of school. A daily letter might have the children start with the following version of a KWL chart. Have them date the very first page in their journals and write "Things I know about second grade." Allow five to ten minutes for them to respond. Expect children to write three or four sentences or phrases. Next, have them write "What would you like to learn in second grade?" Follow that with "What would you like to know about second grade?"

Share the children's responses to each of the questions. Second graders are learning to be better listeners. They love hearing each others' responses. At the end of the school year, they enjoy reflecting on the responses they wrote the first day of school. "What did I learn in second grade?" can be their final entry for the year. On the last two days of school, my students like to pass their journals around the class for autographing.

Are there any good journal examples from literature?

Yes. Look at *My Worst Days Diary* by Suzzane Altman (Bantam, 1995), *Amelia's Notebook* by Marissa Moss (Tricycle Press, 1995), and *The Magic Cornfield* by Nancy Willard (Harcourt Brace, 1997). The first is a good one to share at the beginning of the year. Save the second until mid-year. The last is fun any time. Other books including examples of journals are *Rehema's Journey* by Barbara A. Margolies (Scholastic, 1990), *Learning to Swim in Swahili land* and *Three Days on a River in a Red Canoe*, both by Vera B. Williams (William Morrow & Co., 1981) and *Flip's Fantastic Journal* by Angelo De Sare (Penguin, 1999).

Good Mini-Lessons for Journal Writing

⊙ KWL charts: What do you **K**now? What do you **W**ant to know? What have you **L**earned?

⊙ Journal entries for science observations can determine what mini-lesson is needed. Depending on the work at hand, this may include writing an observation and illustrating it with a diagram. A diagram should include lines, arrows, and correct labeling.

⊙ Descriptive writing

⊙ Expressive writing

⊙ Explaining a math concept

⊙ Writing about weekend activities

⊙ Writing about the week in school

⊙ Writing about a vacation

⊙ Writing about a field trip

⊙ List writing

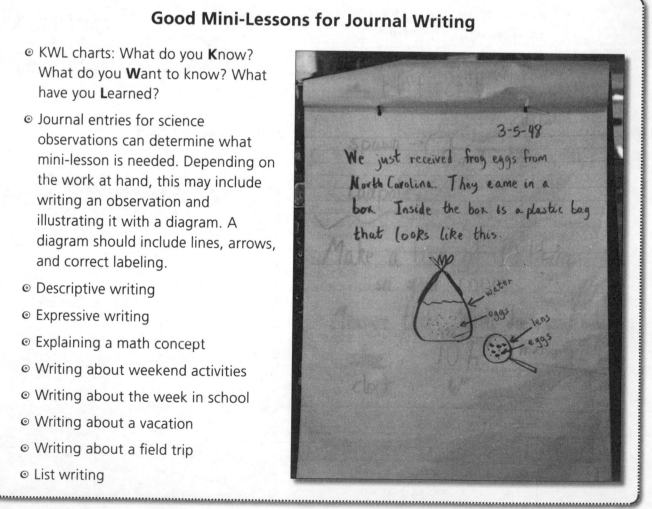

Can second graders write nonfiction or inquiry-based type research?

By the middle of the school year most second graders are fluent enough readers to read from nonfiction resources. These can include Internet sites for children, children's encyclopedias, and many nonfiction trade books that are published at grades 2 to 4 reading levels. It's best to include some nonfiction in your literature collection so that your class has had small group experiences with the form. Additionally, discussions and reading responses can include discussions of how fiction differs from nonfiction.

What are some good subjects for second graders to research?

Ideally, subjects for inquiry-based writing should be based on areas of study students have found extremely interesting. These may include: food, animals, cities, things people do, authors, aspects of their environment, and so on. The Internet and a plethora of nonfiction written at a level suitable for young children provide plenty of resources.

How can children gather and organize the resources?

Children work best when they have an easy way to divide the subject area into smaller areas. A colleague of mine, who taught second grade for 22 years, always had her students research animals by breaking the topic down into the areas of appearance, young, habitat, food, and other facts. Together we used those categories to design a simple research booklet that the children love. Here are directions for this flip booklet:

Research Booklet

MATERIALS

- 3 sheets of different colored copy paper
- 3 sheets of lined writing paper

1 Fold the first color and one sheet of writing paper down 2 inches.

2 Fold the second color and one sheet of writing paper down 3 inches.

3 Fold the third color and one sheet of writing paper down 4 inches.

4. Place the sheets inside each other to form a flip booklet with different lengths of paper showing.

5. Open the booklet and staple it along the fold line with a long-arm stapler.

6. On each of the pieces of colored copy paper that show, write the designated areas of focus.

How can I help students get started with their research?

First, each child needs to choose a subject for his or her flip book. Then the children need guidance to break their subjects into about five areas of focus. A KWL chart can help with the process. Begin with the KW part. Then organize the subject by sorting the statements and questions. Write the areas of focus on the research booklet. The children will need time to find books in the library and check the Internet. Provide guidance as they classify the facts to fit into their format. Some children may need help with reading and writing. I teach mini-lessons on a chart throughout the lesson, modeling the process with my own subject.

Animal Reports

FOOD
What does your animal eat?
How does the animal get its food?
Does the animal store food?

YOUNG
How long is the animal pregnant?
Does the male or female build the nest?
Where is the nest built?
How long before the newborn is on its own?
What is the baby animal called?
How many animals are born at a time?
What do the baby animals eat?
How is the baby animal cared for and taught?

Appearance
What does the animal's body look like?
Does it have fur? What color is the fur?
Does the fur change colors? Ears? Face?
Legs? Feet? Paws? Nose? Snout? Eyes?
Or; does the animal have feathers? Wings?
Wing span?
How much does the animal weigh?
How tall is the animal?

What kind of lesson helps children begin the research process?

Choose a subject. Have the class help break it down into smaller parts, which you record on chart paper. Then read aloud from a book about the subject. Choose a fact and have the children help decide where it should go and how to write it. Do this until there is at least one fact in each of your subject areas. Repeat this process for a few days to gather some facts to use for the next step.

Animal Reports

Puffins   FOOD
eat fish

YOUNG
baby puffins called pufflings
take 2 years to grow

APPEARANCE
not bright colors in winter
dusky gray face
chunky body, short wings   HABITAT

live in the ocean
live in North   from Maine to Canada along
Atlantic
Also live in North Pacific OTHER FACTS

Fly more than 1,000 miles
live 29 years 3 different kinds

How do the children write their gathered facts into a report?

Once the children have gathered enough facts, model what to do next. Read through the facts in one of the small subject areas. Discuss how, for a report on a bird, for example, on the appearance page there are facts about the head, feet, wings, and so on, written in no specific order. Discuss sorting these to write a paragraph. You've probably worked on paragraph writing during reading and writing, and through the daily letter. As the children dictate a topic sentence and two or three more sentences, putting the agreed-upon facts in logical order, write the paragraph on a chart.

What are some ways to show off the finished report?

Have the report typed into a small book at a school publishing center or have the children type or hand-write a final copy with illustrations. Each child will enjoy sharing his or her area of expertise and being the expert for the day on that topic in your class or in other classes.

What is the best way to teach second graders about creative writing?

One of the best ways to teach writing is by using graphic organizers. These might include a character map or a beginning, middle, and end story map. Maps are also great for reading response. (See character map and beginning, middle, and end story map at the end of this chapter.) Sometime around mid-year the children are ready to apply mapping to their own creative writing.

What are some ways to use literature as teaching examples?

Offering examples of good writing from literature is an effective way to teach writing. Reading the story and breaking it down into parts helps to clarify the writing process. You can use literature to emphasize two strong areas of focus for creative writing: a clear beginning, middle, and end, and a problem and solution. Here are three examples:

Just So Stories

Once the children have completed their research reports on animals, they might enjoy writing "Just So Stories," stories of how an animal came to have a particular characteristic. Good examples to read to children include *Why Ducks Sleep on One Leg* by Sherry Garland (Scholastic, 1993), *How Giraffe Got Such a Long Neck* by Michael

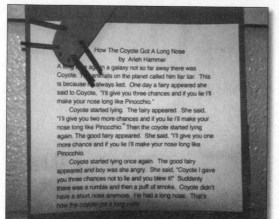

Rosen (Dial Books for Young Readers, 1993), and *Why the Possum's Tail is Bare and Other North American Indian Nature Tales* collected by James E. Connolly (Stemmer House, 1992).

We used a chart (see photo) to construct our own Just So Stories. The stories were displayed to look as if the animals were holding their own tales.

Tales and Small Tales

The next activity's examples use tall tales, which are an American genre, and small tales, stories about little people which are culturally diverse. (See page 98 for a math integration.) You can read stories to the class, and the children can read independently during reading workshop.

The list of possible literary examples is long. (See page 68.) However, two to four examples can get the class started in writing their own tall tales and small tales about themselves.

LESSON 1 TALL TALES

MATERIALS

- ◎ books
- ◎ character maps, story maps (see pages 69–70)
- ◎ pencils
- ◎ writing paper

1 Explain the history of a tall tale. This can be found on the jacket cover or author note in the Steven Kellogg books. Then begin reading the tall tales to and with the children. Discuss reality vs. fantasy, pointing out that these are

tall tales because of the "big lies" or exaggerated truths being told. Emphasize that as the stories left the community in which they happened, the tales grew taller and taller.

2 After reading the first story, discuss and map the beginning/middle/end on the story map and the character on a character map. (Use an overhead or enlarge a map on a chart to fill in as you discuss the character with the children.) The reason these tales are perfect for teaching is that the protaganists' characteristics are so clear, even exaggerated, and tell the story. Repeat the mapping process with at least two stories. Show how the "big lies" make up the middle of the stories as well as most of the detail.

3 Explain to the children that they are going to write a tall tale about themselves. Discuss possibilities of "big lies" they could tell. Use yourself as an example. Map some possibilities with them.

(H) The character map for "big lies" and descriptive detail about the character can be a very creative homework assignment.

4 Model a story by writing your own based on your character map. Map your own story on a story map and character maps with the children. This can even be your letter that day. A few of my students even believed that part of what I wrote was true and asked if it was.

5 Once the children have completed their character maps, have them map a beginning, middle, and end for their story. With these two graphic organizers in front of them the children can write their own story.

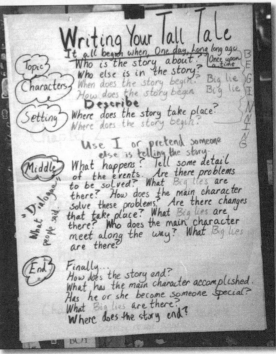

LESSON 2   SMALL TALES

MATERIALS

- character maps
- writing paper for rough drafts
- copies of small tale folding book

These stories about little people may include characters like Thumbelina, Tom Thumb, elves, and leprechauns. There are some multicultural tales, too. For this activity you want the children to come up with a way in which they might have shrunk. You might mention the movie *Honey, I Shrunk the Kids.* Help the children brainstorm for other ways they can shrink, as exemplified in the stories. These may include:

"I was born only one inch tall and only grew to about one foot."

"I am so small that I can only be measured in centimeters."

"My brother put me in the dryer one day."

"I became friendly with an elf."

"I bought a magic meter shrinking shirt. Every time I wear it I shrink to 30 centimeters."

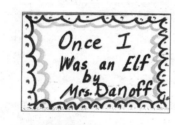

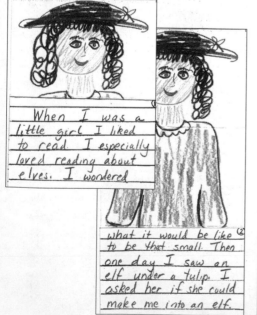

The children's stories will tell their own experiences with being small. These stories are going to be small or short-in-length stories so that they can fit the small-tale fold-up format. These little books can fit in a pocket.

The children's stories should include: how they got small; why they got small; where they were when they got small; who or what made them small; when they got small; what is as small as they are; what they can do now that they are small; what they can't do now that they are small; and anything else they'd like to include.

Writing a short story becomes a challenge for some children who are used to going on and on. Children may wish to make themselves normal size again at the end.

Button Stories

LESSON 1   I FOUND A BUTTON!

MATERIALS

- ◎ buttons
- ◎ writing paper
- ◎ button stories:
  Bone Button Borscht by Aubrey Davis. Kids Can Press, 1995.
  The Button Box by Margarette S. Reid. Penguin, 1995.
  Frog and Toad Are Friends by Arnold Lobel. Harper Trophy, 1970.
  The Yellow Button by Anne Mazer. Random House, 1990.

1 Hide buttons in the classroom.

2 Read a button story.

3 Have a button hunt in the classroom.

4 Discuss possibilities as to where these buttons may have been before and where they may go next.

5 Have children write about their buttons.

6 Glue buttons to the final copy.

What are some ways to teach poetry writing?

Introduce poetry writing by sharing some examples of poetry. Poems are available whether you're writing haiku, pattern poems, rhyming poems, or poems about a particular subject. Many different kinds of subjects are covered by poetry anthologies. In fact, there's probably a poem on just about any subject.

Children enjoy reading and writing poetry because the success is almost instant when properly taught. There are example lessons throughout this book on particular subjects.

Can poetry writing be taught in Writer's Workshop?

Yes. List or pattern poems are best for beginners.

The chart pictured shows a lesson that can be integrated with the animal reports. The children brainstormed words to rhyme with animal body parts and the names of their animals. Then they were instructed to write sentences in which the last word on the line could rhyme with at least one more line, or couplets. Nonsense poems were acceptable and fun to write. These worked beautifully for our geometry projects. (See page 93 in the math chapter.) The *Poetry Place Anthology* from Instructor Books (Scholastic, 1983) is an excellent resource for poems and poetry writing.

What else can children do with their poems and poetry experiences?

Once you have introduced children to poetry, they can copy a poem and illustrate it for a book. Each page can show one line. An example of this is the Susan Jeffers illustration of the Robert Frost poem "Stopping by Woods on a Snowy Evening" (Dutton Children's Books, 1978). Children can follow the same format with one of their own poems.

Children can also make shape books for poetry. Place directions for a shape book and a selection of subject-related poems at the Imagination Station. Or challenge children to find a poem the theme of which fits the shape of the book. This process can enhance and individualize learning about a particular subject.

Included on page 71 is a "Basket of Spring Flowers" shape book template. Children may choose a spring poem and perhaps present the book to their mom or caregiver for Mother's Day. Some possible poems are: "Out in the Hills," from *June is a Tune that Jumps on a Star* by Sarah Wilson (Simon &

Schuster, 1993); "Counting," from *Higgle Wiggle* by Eve Merriam (William Morrow & Co., 1994); "I'm in the Mood for Mud," and "Tree," from *Bing Bang Boing* by Douglas Florian (Penguin, 1996).

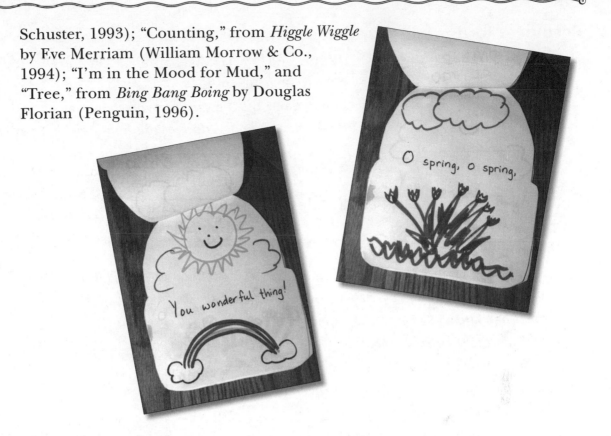

If I tell the class "It's time for Writing Workshop," can I expect them to just start writing?

Children need time to write and to choose their own subjects. As long as the structure is in place and you've presented writing in a nonthreatening way, the class is ready to write.

What if a child can't decide on a subject or get started?

Writers write about their own experiences. Discuss this with the child and encourage him or her to tell you about an event in his or her life. Once the child has verbalized the story, tell him or her that he can write it down in just that way.

A word map is another way to get a story started. Have the child choose a word and draw a bubble around it. Then have him or her draw lines on which to mark ideas associated with that word. Some teachers post story-starter ideas. These are sentences that can begin a story. An example of this is: Once I met a... The other day I found a....

Writing with second graders can include a variety of genres and lessons. They are ready to write. So write on!

Resources for teaching writing

Bromley, Karen, and Linda Irwin-De Vitis, and Marcia Modlo. *Graphic Organizers*. Scholastic, 1995.

Graves, Donald. *A Fresh Look at Writing*. Heinemann, 1994.

Harwayne, Shelley, and Lucy McCormick Caulkins. *The Writing Workshop*. Heinemann, 1987.

Jackson, Norma R. with Paula L.Pillow. *The Reading–Writing Workshop: Getting Started*. Scholastic, 1992.

Sunflower, Cherlyn. *75 Creative Ways to Publish Students' Writing*. Scholastic, 1993.

Just a few tall tales and small tales

Tall Tales

The Bunyans by Audrey Wood. Scholastic, 1996.

I Was Born About 10,000 Years Ago retold by Steven Kellogg. William Morrow, 1996.

Johnny Appleseed retold by Steven Kellogg. William Morrow, 1988.

Larger Than Life by Robert D. San Souci. Bantam Doubleday, 1991.

Mike Fink retold by Steven Kellogg. William Morrow, 1992.

Paul Bunyan retold by Steven Kellogg. William Morrow, 1984.

Pecos Bill retold by Steven Kellogg. William Morrow, 1986.

Pecos Bill by Patsy Jensen. Troll, 1994.

Sally Ann Thunder Ann Whirlwind Crockett retold by Caron Lee Cohen. Greenwillow, 1985.

Sally Ann Thunder Ann Whirlwind Crockett retold by Caron Lee Cohen. William Morrow & Co., 1989.

Sally Ann Thunder Ann Whirlwind Crockett retold by Steven Kellogg. William Morrow, 1995.

Sam and the Tigers by Julius Lester. Penguin, 1996.

Small Tales

The Elves and the Shoemaker by Paul Galdone. Houghton Mifflin, 1984.

The Inch Boy by Junko Morimoto. Penguin, 1984.

John Henry by Julius Lester. Penguin, 1994.

The Rainbabies by Laura Kraus Melmed. William Morrow, 1992.

Teeny Tiny retold by Jill Bennet. Oxford, 1986.

Thumbelina by Hans Christian Anderson. Penguin, 1979.

Tim O'Toole and the Wee Folk by Gerald McDermott. Penguin, 1990.

Tom Thumb by Richard Jesse Watson. Harcourt Brace Jovanovich, 1989.

The Teeny Tiny Teacher by Stephanie Calmensin. Scholastic, 1998.

The Toy Brother by William Steig. HarperCollins, 1998.

Albert Goes to Town by Jennifer Jordan. Chronicle Books, 1997.

Tall and Small Tale

Jim and the Beanstalk by Raymond Briggs. The Putnam Grosset Group, 1970.

Name_____ Date_____

Story Map

Title:_____

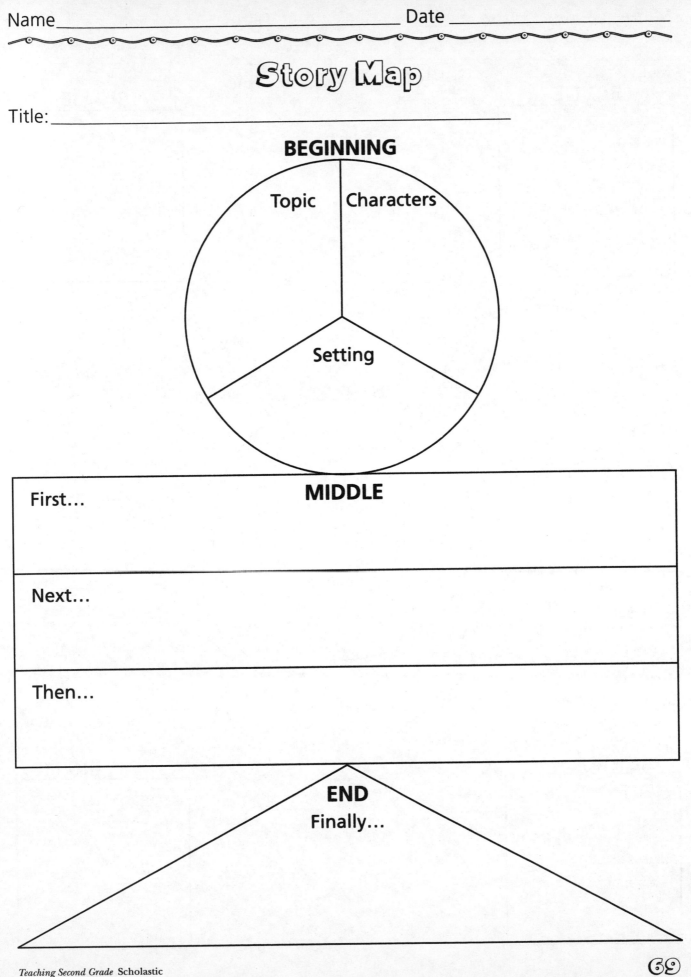

BEGINNING

Topic | Characters

Setting

MIDDLE

First...

Next...

Then...

END
Finally...

Name_____ Date _____

Character Map

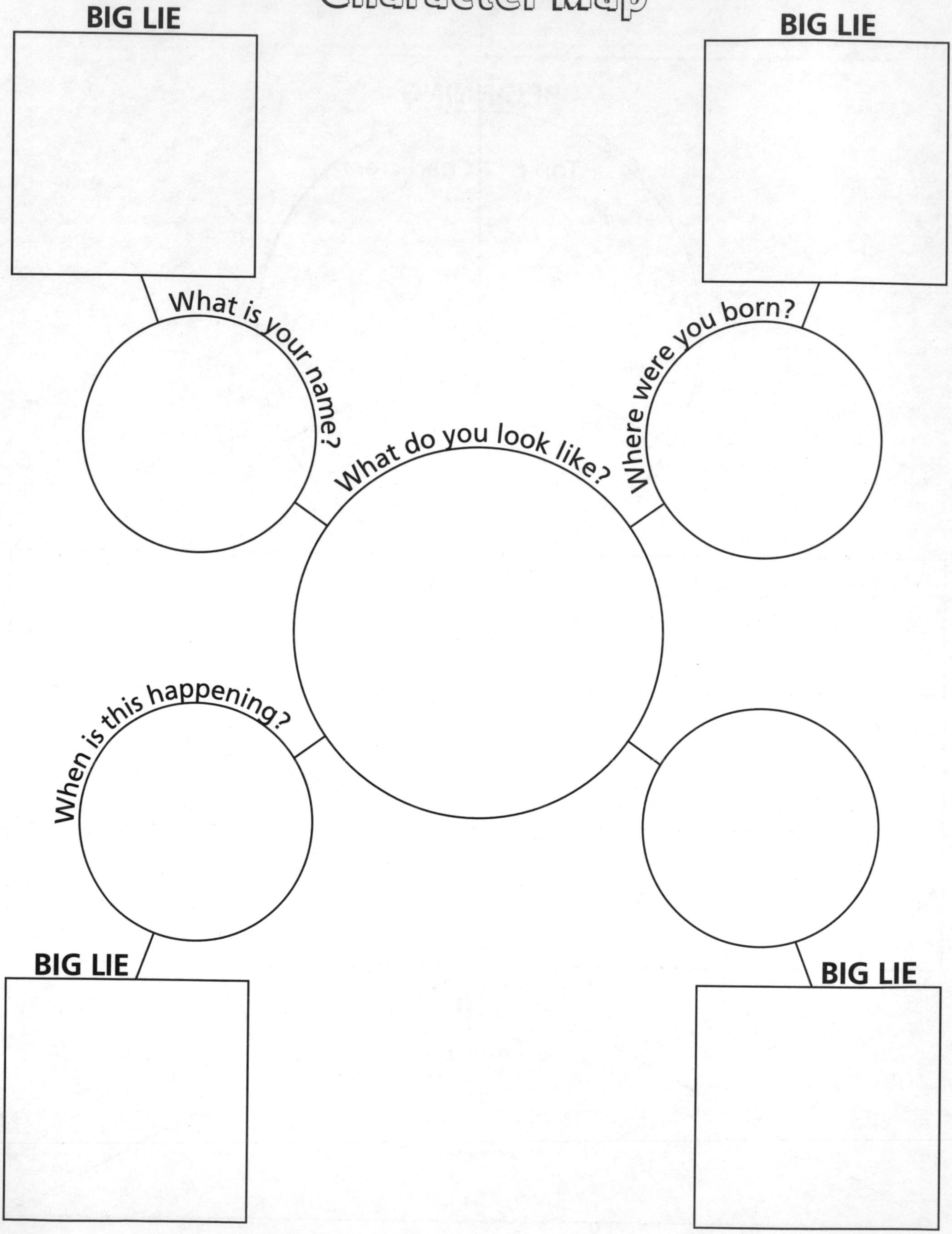

BIG LIE

BIG LIE

What is your name?

Where were you born?

What do you look like?

When is this happening?

BIG LIE

BIG LIE

Teaching Second Grade Scholastic

Spring Basket Template

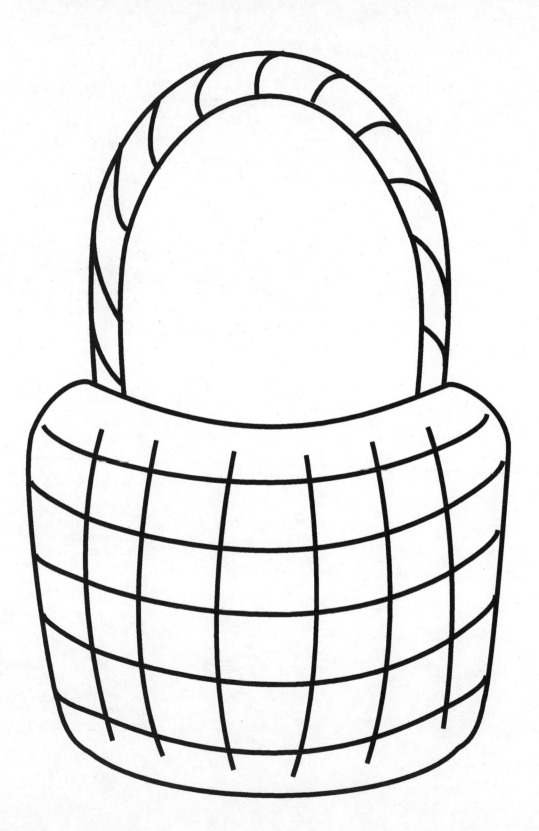

CHAPTER 6

Spelling

Almost the very first question asked in second grade is,

"How do you spell …?"

The answer invariably is "Sound it out" or "Can you find the word in the room?" or "Don't worry about spelling it the book way now." These are all good answers. The real question for the teacher now is "How do you move your students from phonetic or transitional spelling to correct spelling?" Part of the answer must lie in the age of the children. If learning to read is the phenomenon of first grade, then learning to spell is the phenomenon of second grade.

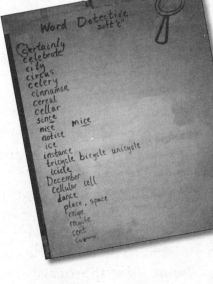

Is there a range of spelling awareness and skill?

Is there ever! It's amazing. Some children have something like a photographic memory. They actually enter second grade spelling almost every word correctly. Others can still be misspelling their own names by not writing them as proper nouns. The average second grader has some correct spelling under his or her belt and is very willing and able to learn quite a bit more as the year progresses. It really is phenomenal!

Does spelling count?

We all asked that question at some time or another. The answer is most definitely a big YES! In second grade it really does. It's up to you, the teacher, to make it do so. Children's writing—anybody's writing for that matter—is not literate unless the spelling is correct. High-frequency words are especially noticeable. Spelling a word like *they* incorrectly can stick with a child all the way through high school. Fortunately, computer spell-check programs will catch that one. However, homonyms are quite tricky, even for a computer.

Is there a specific spelling program to use?

Your district may have specified a particular program. Check there first. If you're looking for a spelling program yourself, Zaner Bloser publishes one that is based on the work of Jerry Zutell from Ohio State University. This technique employs a word-sort approach. Included in this chapter are some activities based on this approach that have worked for me. (For further reading, see Zutell, Jerry, (1996). "The Directed Spelling Thinking Activity Providing an Effective Balance in Word Study Instruction," *The Reading Teacher* Vol. 50, No. 2. 98-108.)

What kinds of classroom scaffolding encourage correct spelling?

Dictionaries are very important. Have a number of children's intermediate dictionaries on hand. Also, be sure to have adult or college editions available. Teaching the children how to use the dictionary as soon as possible will help to improve their spelling skills.

Keep an alphabetized list of the high-frequency words (see the list on page 79) posted for quick and ready reference. There are also words that children frequently misspell or periodically use and want to have spelled for them. Post those in a special area and add to the list as the year goes by. When you're studying a particular theme, post appropriate words on a chart for quick reference.

Children can also keep their own lists on the last two pages of their personal journals, in their reading journals, or in their spelling journals.

How can second graders improve their spelling skills?

Second graders are quite aware that there is correct spelling. That's why they ask. They can improve their skills if they're encouraged to find the spelling on their own, to self-edit, and mostly to realize that it's time to improve. Classroom and homework activities can reinforce the skills.

Should the teacher correct every word that a child misspells?

That's an individual decision. I pick and choose—especially at the beginning of the year. It can be very distressing to a child to see his or her paper all marked up with spelling corrections. What you decide also depends upon the individual child and what the child is writing.

For a final copy of a written piece, the answer is: Yes!, be sure all the words are spelled correctly. For a reading response in a reading notebook, a word that is right in front of a child, require that he or she copy it correctly. Transferring correct spelling is very important. If it is, or has been, a spelling word, have the child self-correct. Remember, though, to start out slow and easy. Accept more mistakes until you get to know the children and have established expectations and procedures.

Is it wise to give a weekly pretest and test?

Frankly, I'm torn about giving a weekly test. Children are always going to be tested, and this can be a place to start that practice. However, the tensions built up in anticipation of the test can run high—even for second graders and their parents. Besides, the first time a child writes a word, he or she may write it incorrectly and start a habit that can be hard to break. The real test of learning a spelling word is to write it correctly after the test. You may want to try dictations and cloze activities instead of "list" tests.

What if there is no district spelling program?

Children can have individual spelling notebooks or journals in which they keep their weekly list, individual lists, and write their homework activities. Each child will fill a 100-page, hardcover composition book by the end of the school year. You might take the weekly list from a list of high-frequency words like the one on page 79.

You may use a list that draws from the vocabulary of lessons or units currently being studied in math, science, or social studies. Individual lists that review high-frequency words and lists with spelling patterns are good choices. Or children's individual lists can be words they want to work on or frequently misspell. Use a list of about eight to ten words each week and extend it with a word sort activity (see below).

What kinds of activities can the whole class work on?

There are so many, including word sorts and word detectives.

Word Sort

Jerry Zutell's article in *The Reading Teacher* (see page 74) includes a number of word-search activities similar to the following:

MATERIALS

- ◎ sentence strips in two colors
- ◎ a pocket chart
- ◎ chart paper
- ◎ individual student notebooks
- ◎ markers, pencils

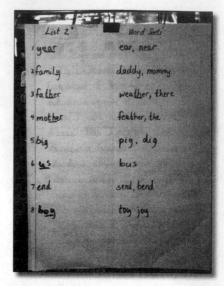

1 Tell students you are going to begin learning about words.

2 Show them how to set up their notebook for two columns, as pictured above.

3 Instruct the class not to write the word until it is on the chart because the class is going to spell the word together.

4 Say the word—*moon*, for example. Ask what letters the children hear and have the class predict how to spell the word. Predictions may vary.

5 Ask the children why they think the word would be spelled that way. Possible answers include:

> I can hear the *m* at the beginning and the *n* at the end.
>
> I know *oo* goes …
>
> I've seen it spelled that way.
>
> It rhymes with June and my birthday is in June. (for a misspelling)
>
> I can hear a *u*. (for a misspelling)
>
> A cow goes "moo" and I know how to spell *moo.*
>
> It sounds like the word *blue.* And I can see the word *blue* on the color chart over there. (for a misspelling)

6 Tell the children that all their ideas are good. Then write the letters on one color of sentence strip. Place the word on a chart. Have the children say and spell the word together and then write it in their spelling journals.

7 Ask the children what they think might be special about the way this word is spelled, based on their other ideas. Encourage the response of the *oo* sound. Underline the *oo*. Note: You could also work on words that end with *n* or begin with *m* for a simpler lesson.

8 For the word sort, ask if the children can think of other words that have the *oo* sound that sounds the same as in *moon*. Children will name some that do and some that do not. Respond to and spell each word—for instance, *do, moo, tune, cocoon, noon, stew.*

9 Choose two to four additional words with the same spelling pattern to write on another color sentence strip. Place these words in the word sort column. Have the children do the same in their spelling notebooks.

Repeat this process for each word. The children will end up with a spelling list and a bonus list. It may take some coaxing, encouragement, and teacher ideas at first to help students understand and discover spelling patterns, but it's well worth it. Very quickly, children will enter the classroom in the morning talking about other words they've found. Encourage them to write those words in their notebooks in the right place.

At the end of the week, if you're giving a spelling test, test the children on the list words first. Then have them turn their papers over to write the word sorts. The results I've observed when I've used this technique have been excellent and very exciting. Word sorts help children understand our language better, and they love learning to spell this way.

Word Detective

Sometimes you and the children will notice an unusual spelling pattern when it's not time for a spelling lesson. However, there's always time for a spelling lesson with a word-detective chart available. For example, when you notice spellings such as *ic* as in *terrific* or soft *c* as in *circle*, start a chart with one word and ask the children to be Word Detectives and to be on the lookout for words with the same pattern or letter sounds.

Children will enjoy adding to the list whenever they hear or see a word with the pattern they're looking for. This may happen at any time—during the daily letter, reading or writing time, and so on. Be prepared for the excitement of discovery.

How about homonyms?

Children love homonyms. These words are as fascinating as they are confusing. Keep a homonym list available on chart paper, and change it as you go. Encourage children to make their own copy of the homonyms in their spelling notebook or personal journal. *The King Who Rained* by Fred Gywnne (Simon & Schuster, 1970) can get the class started learning about homonyms with a big laugh.

How about suffixes?

Explain to the children about root words and how suffixes change them. Place examples in a pocket chart so that children can move endings and root words around. While working on the daily letter, have the children circle root words and suffixes.

What are some spelling homework activities?

Children can keep their spelling homework organized and the spelling words handy for review by using a spelling notebook or journal. You can have them take the journal home each day to work on activities such as the following. (Activities such as spelling crossword puzzles or word searches can be stapled onto the children's notebook pages.)

- alphabetizing words
- adding more words to word sorts
- writing each word in a sentence
- completing and creating crossword and/or word-search puzzles (see pages 80–82)
- writing a definition for each word using the dictionary
- writing a three-hint riddle for each word
- adding suffixes when possible
- finding sentences in newspapers that include the words
- making a word map for the word
- creating a pictorial representation of the word

Spelling is one of those controversial subjects. How to teach it is constantly being written about, debated, and discussed. Nevertheless, second graders are ready to enjoy the challenge and process of acquiring spelling skills.

Resources for teaching spelling

Bolton, Faye and Diane Snowball.*Teaching Spelling: A Practical Resource.* Heinemann, 1993.

Gentry, J. Richard *Spel ... is a Four-Letter Word.* Heinemann, 1987.

Hong, Min and Patty Stafford. *Spelling Strategies that Work.* Scholastic Professional Books, 1997.

Sight Words/High-Frequency Words

about	did	him	mother	run	too
after	do	his	much	said	took
again	down	home	my	saw	two
all	eat	house	name	school	under
also	end	how	need	see	until
always	ever	if	never	she	up
am	every	in	new	should	upon
an	family	into	next	sister	us
and	father	is	nice	small	very
another	fell	it	night	so	walk
any	find	just	no	some	want
are	first	knew	not	soon	was
around	for	know	now	started	way
as	friend	last	of	take	we
ask	from	left	off	tell	well
at	fun	let	old	ten	went
back	gave	like	on	than	were
be	get	little	once	that	what
because	girl	live	one	the	when
been	give	long	only	their	where
before	go	look	or	them	which
best	going	lot	other	then	who
big	good	love	our	there	why
boy	got	mad	out	these	will
brother	had	made	over	they	with
but	happy	man	people	thing	work
by	has	many	place	think	would
called	have	may	play	this	year
came	he	me	put	though	yes
can	heard	men	ran	through	you
come	help	money	really	time	your
could	her	more	ride	to	
day	here	most	right	told	

Word List

1. _____
2. _____
3. _____
4. _____
5. _____
6. _____

7. _____
8. _____
9. _____
10. _____
11. _____
12. _____

Word Search Puzzle

Teaching Second Grade Scholastic

How to Make a Spelling Word Crossword Puzzle

1. Have the spelling words in front of you.

2. Write the words on the blank puzzle below, across, and down. **Keep trying. You do not need to have the same number of words across as down.**

3. Number the words. Try to stay in order.

4. Color in the unused squares.

5. Copy the puzzle onto the blank puzzle leaving the word letters blank, but coloring in the unused squares.

6. Write the hints for *across* and *down*.

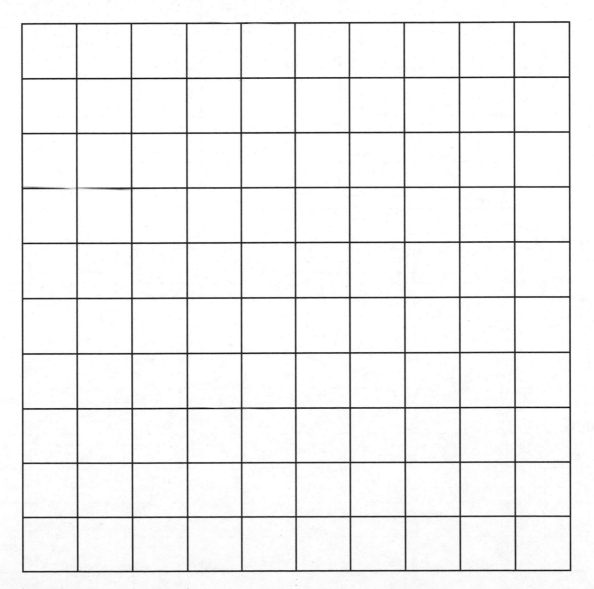

Spelling Word Crossword Puzzle

Across _____

_____

_____

_____

_____

Down _____

_____

_____

_____

_____

CHAPTER 7

Math

As with reading and writing, second graders are ready, willing, and able to apply and learn more about math skills. Most children will say they love math. Some especially love math more than reading and writing. Working on basic concepts and extending the application is very possible with second graders.

What do second graders know about math?

Generally, second graders understand addition. They have a good grasp of the concept of subtraction. They really need to learn and practice the math facts through 18. They'll ask the teacher (and anybody else who is handy) at least five times a day, "What time is it?" They've heard about multiplication and division. Second graders may know what half of something is. They may even know that a pizza pie can be divided into six or eight slices. They love patterns and can be encouraged to extend that knowledge. Though they may have begun place value in first grade, they really don't remember enough to go right into double-digit equations because they're not quite sure about how to handle regrouping. They may remember the words "a package of ten and a package of one hundred."

Second graders may have touched a ruler in first grade. They may know how tall they are. They may have done experiments and cooked with cups. Second graders for the most part know the names of geometric shapes. Some know about the value of coins, but it's rare if any know about the decimal point needed for the dollar value. They're not quite sure which way or where the cent sign goes. But by the end of second grade they do know quite a bit more than when they began!

What are the NCTM standards?

There are 13 standards for K–4. These are:

- Mathematics as problem solving
- Mathematics as communication
- Mathematics as reasoning
- Mathematics as connections
- Estimation
- Number sense and numeration
- Concepts of whole number operations
- Whole number computation
- Geometry and spatial sense
- Measurement
- Statistics and probability
- Fractions
- Patterns and relationships

In setting standards the NCTM's goal was to:

Create a coherent vision of what it means to be mathematically literate both in a world that relies on calculators and computers to carry out mathematical procedures and in a world where mathematics is rapidly growing and is extensively being applied in diverse fields.

Further, NCTM states that:

The intent of this goal is that students will become mathematically literate. This term denotes an individual's ability to explore and conjecture, and to reason logically, as well as to use a variety of mathematical methods effectively to solve problems. By becoming literate, their mathematical power should develop.

—From the NCTM Commission on Standards for School Mathematics (NCTM, 1997)

How do these apply to second grade?

Basically, applying NCTM standards in the classroom means going beyond paper-and-pencil tasks. Explore, conjecture, and reason using a variety of mathematical methods, and encourage, provide, and allow for these opportunities in the classroom.

It's easy to simply follow the program the school or district has adopted, which typically comes from a publisher like Addison Wesley, Steck-Vaughn, Scott Foresman, and others. These programs are textbook-based, and come with a teaching guide, blackline masters, and a student workbook. Chances are good that they follow the NCTM standards and cover the necessary requirements, vocabulary, and methods. Therefore, reviewing the provided materials will help you go beyond them.

Do second-grade classrooms need manipulative math materials?

Yes. Teaching with manipulative math materials encourages a more thorough understanding of concepts. In addition, using an overhead projector and transparencies makes it easier to demonstrate these concepts to the whole class. Using the overhead makes the concept more exciting, too. Children love this medium. Don't forget to use real objects—the clock in the room, change from the teacher's and the children's wallets, and so on. (See page 17 for a list of math supplies.)

What is a reasonable amount of time to spend teaching math each day?

It's a good idea to schedule about 30 to 60 minutes a day for math. This might include teaching and practicing the lesson, computer games, integrations (see Chapter 12), literature extensions, homework correction and explanation, and so on. You may spend more time if you're developing an integration or text set. You may also spend additional time on math when you use a daily letter to teach concepts.

What are some independent math activities?

Having a math-game time can give children the opportunity to work together or independently on computer or board games. It also provides time for you to work with small groups for enrichment or support.

Another possibility is to set up an activity at the Imagination Station. This might include a set of simple directions using some of the materials stored there. Here are two possibilities—Design a Game Board and Tessellations. (See Teacher References on page 99 for books about math that include more ideas.)

Design a Game Board

This idea grew from an idea one of my colleagues shared with me and replicated for my class. She had designed a game (with game board) called "Create a Creature" to reinforce addition and subtractions skills. Players shake the dice, write the two numbers as an addition or subtraction problem, perform the function, and then move that number of spaces around the board. If a child's marker lands on one of the creature's body parts—an arm, a leg, or a nose, for example, the child gets to add that part to his or her creature. I easily created the same game for my students.

The children in my class loved the game and wondered if I'd made the game board myself. It was then that I realized the children could create their own games as well and each make their own copy to take home to play and practice math skills. It also occurred to me that the children could create game boards based on a variety of themes, such as "Build a Mall," "Make a Toy Store," "Make an Aquarium," "Build a Town," "Make a Circus," and so on. You and the children can draw, use stickers, or cut things from magazines to create your game boards.

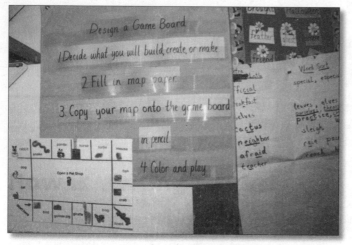

MATERIALS

- © colored pencils, crayons, or markers
- © Game Map (see blank sample on page 101) on which to design a first draft of the game board. (Check each plan feasibility and spelling.)
- © 12" x 18" white tag board on which to transfer the plan for the finished game board. Laminate after game board is created. (If you don't have laminating equipment, the game board can be drawn on a smaller size of lightweight tag and covered with clear contact paper.)
- © List of rules. The following can be adapted to the theme of any game.
    1. Decide whether you are playing with addition, subtraction, or by the sign shown on the die. Roll dice.
    2. Add or subtract numbers on game paper to determine how many spaces you can move. Remember, when subtracting, the higher number is written first. Example: You roll 2 and 7. Write 7 – 2 = 5.
    3. Count and move to land on the space indicated by the roll of the dice. For the example, you would move 5 spaces.

4. Draw on your game paper the part indicated in the space you land on.

5. Continue around the game board until you complete the figure or object you are creating.

6. The first one to complete his or her figure or object wins.

⊚ Unifix cubes; or numbered, dotted, or + or - dice as markers

⊚ Game Paper (see page 102), on which students can write their equations and complete the figure or object they are drawing.

My students enjoy playing their math games independently at school and at home with family members. This is a great way to make math practice fun.

Tessellations

Tessellations are patterns that fit together and repeat. They are available in a number of styles as manipulative materials for math. After children have had hands-on experience with tessellation manipulative materials, they can trace a page of tessellations and then create and color their own designs. This activity takes time and patience.

MATERIALS

⊚ tessellation patterns cut from tag (see sample patterns on page 103)

⊚ 12" x 18" drawing paper

⊚ colored pencils, crayons, or markers

What is appropriate for math homework and practice?

Be sure you give practice homework that has children practice skills you've already taught them. For example, if you devote a math lesson to place value, then give place-value homework that reinforces what the students learned in class. Most math programs include homework and practice sheets, but practice workbooks are also available in educational stores. You can also create your own practice sheets designed to support your students' needs. In addition, students can make up their own practice sheets to exchange with one another.

What are some ways to extend, enrich, and integrate math skills?

See the list of math resources written just for this purpose at the end of this chapter. Also, many trade books, fiction, and nonfiction develop mathematical concepts. (See page 100 for a list of these.) Depending on how the story you read to the children is told, you can stop and discuss the math as you read or go back over the concepts after you've finished reading.

If the story builds addition concepts as it unfolds, you might rewrite the numbers on a chart and add them with your class. If, on the other hand, the concept is not clear until the end, it's best to wait until you've read the whole story. Still another possibility is to break the book into parts—and possibly more than one math session—and go over math concepts respectively.

What are some math-extension activities to try?

Another way to use books to teach math concepts is to find several books to use as part of a text set to focus on a concept. Using a text set will enable you to develop an extended activity or project to enrich, explore, and apply the concept. This technique adds excitement and extends thinking. (See Chapter 11 for more on Text Sets.)

Following is a text set on time. (See page 97 for one on linear measurement and page 93 for one on geometry.) Children use time in their daily lives. Telling time is considered a part of learning measurement—how the year, month, day, and hour are measured. The fundamental concepts about time that can be examined on an analog clock include:

- the function of the minute hand
- the function of the hour hand
- that 60 minutes equal 1 hour
- that there are 24 hours in a day
- the relationship of numbers on the clock to the minutes they represent
- intervals of time such as quarter past and of the hour, half past the hour, a.m. and p.m., noon, and midnight.

Understanding these concepts enables children to read analog and digital clocks.

Telling Time: The Creepy Clock Café

The Creepy Clock Café text-set lessons apply concepts children are learning about time. The following text groupings and lessons will help children connect the time concepts to people and parties and Halloween. You can rename the café if you do not want to use a Halloween theme. For example, you might call it "Round the Clock" café or "Talking Clock" café.

LESSON 1 — INTRODUCTION TO TELLING TIME

When you're beginning to teach time, give the children individual clocks to set, while demonstrating with a clock transparency on the overhead or a larger teacher clock. Start with the hour hand, minute hand, and minutes, going around the clock. Set clocks on the hour and then on the half hour. Name a time, and have a student come up to the transparency to draw the hands correctly on the clock while the rest of the class sets their individual clocks. Remember to use the clock on the wall in your room, too. You can stop at intervals during the day to review times.

LESSON 2 — LARGE-GROUP SHARED READING

Read the book *Clocks and More Clocks* by Pat Hutchins (Macmillan, 1970). Discuss clocks and watches children might have in their homes.

Ⓗ For homework, hand out copies of the Home-Time paper (see page 107) and tell the children how to complete it at home by checking and recording times on clocks and watches. Tell them to find as many clocks or appliances that give the time as they can. Students have fun searching through their homes for clocks.

Each day before beginning work on telling time, review what the students have learned and then continue with new lessons. Use practice worksheets from your math program.

LESSON 3 — LARGE-GROUP SHARED READING

Reinforce the concepts you've taught by reading *The Grouchy Ladybug* by Eric Carle (Harper Trophy, 1986). As you read the book, have the children set their clocks. Follow up with a practice paper on which the children draw hands on clocks or read the time.

LESSON 4 LARGE-GROUP SHARED READING TO BEGIN CONSTRUCTING THE CREEPY CLOCK CAFÉ

MATERIALS

- 4 copies of the clocks and bubbles page (pages 104–105)
- 18" x 6" white construction paper
- 1 copy of the Creepy Clock Café template (page 106)
- 2 different colored pieces of 12"x 18" construction paper
- a paper fastener
- 1-hour hand and 1-minute hand cut from tag board
- a T square or ruler
- glue
- a pencil and colored pencils
- teacher model (See directions below to construct your own.)

This is called the Creepy Clock Café because the clocks are talking about who is arriving when. That's why the talk bubbles are glued above the clocks.

Start by reading *8 O'Clock* by Jill Creighton (Scholastic, 1995) and having children set their individual clocks to match the times in the story. The story is about people arriving at a restaurant in time for dinner or a party. Then explain to the children that they'll be writing a time storybook too.

Make a sample flap book, as described below, and show and read it to the class.

1. Direct the children to fold the 18" x 6" white paper in half lengthwise. Show them how to glue it lengthwise to one end of one of the 12" x 18" pieces of colored construction paper. The fold is placed along the center of the paper so that the open end becomes the bottom of the page. Model this process for your class.

2 Pair the children to work cooperatively to trace the template on the other color of construction paper.

3 Glue this to the previously glued piece, leaving the other end open, but gluing the café tracing on top so that white paper is seen only when the bottom is folded up.

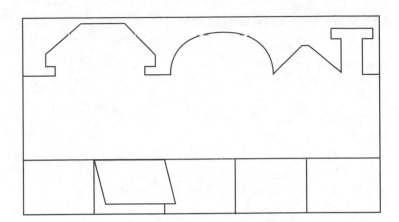

4 Have the children fold open the white paper and use a T square to draw a horizontal line 1" down from the top.

5 Then have them place a ruler along bottom edge and mark off $3\frac{1}{2}$" intervals. The last space should measure 4". The children should then draw lines to intersect the line marked across top.

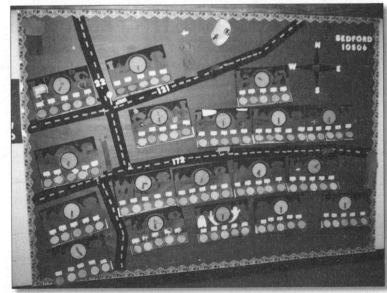

6 Model carefully cutting through the white and color on top to create flaps. Have the children make their cuts.

7 Have the children cut out small clocks and glue one on top of each door. Have them glue the large clock onto the center.

8 Punch a hole in the center of the large clock to attach the hands with a paper fastener.

LESSON 5   WRITING THE STORY

Brainstorm ideas for writing the story. Include the occasion—birthday party, Halloween, family reunion—and characters arriving—friends, vampires, ghosts, uncle, aunt, and so on. Have children flip up pages and write on lines who arrived, and then illustrate below.

Halloween Example

IN BUBBLE	IN FLIPPED-UP DOOR
At 4:00 p.m.	Two ghosts arrived.
At 6:00 p.m.	Three witches arrived.
At 9:00 p.m.	Four vampires arrived.
At 11:00 p.m.	Five pumpkins arrived.
By 12:00 a.m.	Everyone was ready for a happy Halloween.

(H) For homework hand out copies of the clock and bubble sheet to each child. Have the children write and draw the times they will be using in their story. Be sure to direct their attention to a.m. and p.m., encouraging them to begin the story in the morning and end the story in the evening. Build in challenge by having the children choose times other than on the hour or half hour— 10:47 a.m. or 1:18 p.m., for example.

LESSON 6   WRITING THE STORY CONTINUES

1 Check homework and then have the children use their times to write on the talk bubbles, "At [insert time]."

2 Have the children cut and glue their word bubbles above the clocks, then draw hands on clocks to correspond to the times in the bubbles. The story is complete.

Children enjoy sharing their stories and comparing times. The large clock with the spinning hands can also be used for more time-setting practice.

Assessment Tip

⊙ Write times on another copy of the blank clocks page.

⊙ Can the children fill in times on blank clocks?

⊙ Using the clock in your room, ask children the time periodically throughout the day. Repeat this on a weekly basis to practice and reinforce skills.

LESSONS 7 AND 8
HOMEWORK MENU AND STORY PROBLEM

(H) Just for fun, make a Creepy Clock Café Menu. Design one to model for the class. Then have children create their own menus. Request that prices be kept to under 20¢. On the following day, share the menus. Then have the children write story problems using their menus. The next day, have the children share their story problems. Continue menu math by having the children design menus throughout the year. Pictured are a sample menu and story problem.

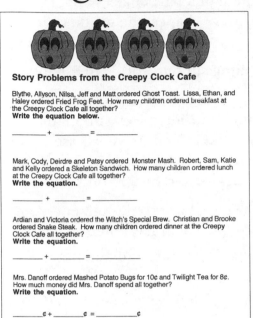

Story Problems from the Creepy Clock Cafe

Blythe, Allyson, Nilsa, Jeff and Matt ordered Ghost Toast. Lissa, Ethan, and Haley ordered Fried Frog Feet. How many children ordered breakfast at the Creepy Clock Cafe all together?
Write the equation below.

_____ + _____ = _____

Mark, Cody, Deirdre and Patsy ordered Monster Mash. Robert, Sam, Katie and Kelly ordered a Skeleton Sandwich. How many children ordered lunch at the Creepy Clock Cafe all together?
Write the equation.

_____ + _____ = _____

Ardian and Victoria ordered the Witch's Special Brew. Christian and Brooke ordered Snake Steak. How many children ordered dinner at the Creepy Clock Cafe all together?
Write the equation.

_____ + _____ = _____

Mrs. Danoff ordered Mashed Potato Bugs for 10¢ and Twilight Tea for 8¢. How much money did Mrs. Danoff spend all together?
Write the equation.

_____ ¢ + _____ ¢ = _____ ¢

Geometry and Spatial Sense: Animals Come in All Sorts of Shapes and Sizes

Geometry is more that just recognizing shapes. Second graders can explore, experiment with, visualize, draw, and compare shapes in various ways. They can reproduce the shapes of objects from the world in which we live. Their spatial understanding can be developed by arranging and rearranging shapes and exploring how shapes change. They can cut paper shapes and make new shapes from the parts. A list of books that explore shapes is found on page 100.

MATERIALS

- chart paper or overhead projector
- shapes cut from tagboard
- manipulative fraction circles, tangrams, fraction squares
- a variety of colored construction paper
- pencils, markers
- scissors, ruler, compass
- glue

LESSON 1   WHAT DO YOU KNOW?

1 Find out what your students know about the word *geometry*.

2 Have the children name and describe shapes. Look around the room. Ask the children if they see anything that reminds them of a particular shape. For example, the globe is a sphere, pattern blocks are shapes, the windows are rectangles, the tables are rectangles.

3 Discuss how shapes represent and describe things in our world (the shape of our heads, a bus, wheels, a building).

4 Have the children name things or parts of things outside the classroom that remind them of a shape (a truck's body is a rectangle, and its wheels are circles; pies and cookies are circles; pizza is cut into triangle-shaped pieces; a sandwich is square and can be cut into rectangles or triangles; and on and on).

5 On a chart or on an overhead, trace around shapes, having children guess and describe as you do. Ask about corners and sides. As you trace, children may say:

- That looks like a circle because you are going all around and not stopping.

- You're making one corner, another corner, oh three corners! That's a triangle.

- That's one corner, two corners…oh three sides up to another corner and another. That has five sides. (Teacher responds by naming a pentagon.)

6 Trace and name triangle, rectangle, square, circle, ellipse, oval, pentagon, hexagon, and octagon. Then ask the questions again about shapes in the room and outside. A stop sign is sure to come up.

7 Give the children a piece of unlined paper and have them draw and name shapes. If your math program has blackline masters addressing geometry, use these as well.

LESSON 2   LARGE-GROUP SHARED READING AND MANIPULATIVE MATH MATERIALS

1 Read *The Shape of Things* by Dayle Ann Dodds (Candlewick Press, 1994). Allow plenty of time for reflection and enjoyment.

2 Give each child a 12" x 18" piece of construction paper to use as a mat and a variety of manipulative math materials. Be sure each child understands that he or she must keep his or her set of materials on the mat. Otherwise you'll have chaos keeping the sets in their original groupings.

3 Encourage the children to explore combining and arranging the shapes on their mats to create a picture. Be sure to encourage the children to look at what their classmates have created.

LESSON 3 PIECES OF SHAPES

Revisit your chart of shapes. Discuss symmetry. Illustrate by drawing a line down the center of a shape to see if it is the same on both sides.

Continue by having the children come up to the chart to draw more of these lines, dividing the shapes into more pieces.

Give the children paper shapes to trace, fold, and cut so that they can have a hands-on experience with this process.

Provide rulers to give the children experience with linear measurement. Have them arrange (not glue) shapes on paper. Have them take these shapes home to experiment with.

Read *Picture Pie 2* by Ed Emberly (Little, Brown & Co., 1996) to encourage ideas for the following assignment.

LESSON 4 LARGE-GROUP SHARED READING AND MANIPULATIVE MATH MATERIALS

Read *Color Zoo* by Lois Ehlert (HarperCollins, 1989). Tell the children you want them to get more specialized now in using the geometric shapes to create. Follow procedures described for lesson 2, but this time expect each child to create an animal with his or her shapes.

You may wish to integrate this activity with an animal-research report (see page 59). You may also wish to read *Grandfather Tang's Story* by Ann Tomper (Crown Publishers, 1990), and have the children experiment with using only tangrams and construction paper to illustrate *Grandfather Tang's Story*. I've had great success with this activity.

> **Assessment Tip**
>
> To assess, have children make a map or small representation of how they can make an animal using shapes. This can be a Ⓗ homework assignment, too. You can give the children a copy of a shape sheet to use at home, reminding them of the possibilities. Be sure to encourage them to use fractions of circles and pieces of shapes.

LESSON 5   CREATING AN ANIMAL FROM PAPER

1. Provide the children with shape templates in various sizes, construction paper, pencils, scissors, and glue.

2. Tell them that now they're ready to plan and create an animal from all sorts of shapes and sizes. It is fun to use brightly colored paper rather than going for a more realistic representation. Encourage them to include more detail using smaller shapes.

3. Have the children create a small map of their more sophisticated animal.

4. Have them trace, cut, and glue together the construction paper to create an animal based on their map.

    These shape-animals make a great bulletin board display and can be used to show off animal poems, too. (See Writing Poetry page 65.)

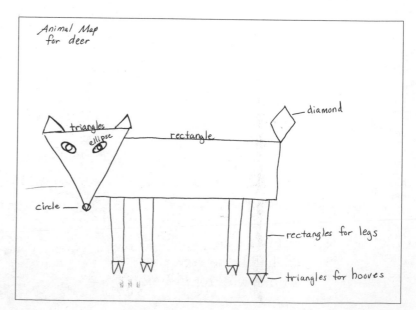

Linear Measurement

By second grade, children are aware that they are measured at the doctor's office and that they are growing. They enjoy walking up to a growth chart and measuring themselves. It's a natural to teach inches and feet by having children measure themselves. The fun part is to have them reproduce the measurements.

MATERIALS

- measurement books (See page 100.)
- Measure Yourself homework paper (See page 108.)
- 2 pieces of 22" x 28" white tag/poster board for each child
- rulers
- scissors
- crayons
- glue

LESSON 1 — LARGE-GROUP SHARED READING

Read one of the measurement books to help begin a discussion about measuring. Give every child a ruler. Go over the inches side and discuss that the ruler is one foot long.

LESSON 2 — HANDS-ON MEASURING

Have the children work in pairs to brainstorm a list of ten objects in the room, write the names of the objects on separate pieces of paper, and work together to measure and record the measurements of each object.

(H) Have each child make a list and measure ten things in his or her room, recording the measurements. Loan children a school ruler if they don't have rulers at home.

LESSON 3 — MEASURE YOURSELF

(H) Hand out the Measure Yourself homework sheet on page 108. Explain to the children that they will need help at home to complete the paper. Go over each area to be measured. Be sure to explain to the children that they are to pretend they are flat, like the paper. Check these papers to be sure they are completed reasonably.

LESSON 4   USING BODY MEASUREMENTS TO CREATE SELF-PORTRAITS

1. Have each child glue the two sheets of tag board together lengthwise with a 1-inch overlap. Allow a few minutes for drying. If necessary, rearrange the room to expand the work space.

2. Instruct the children to use a ruler to measure 1 inch down from the top of the tag board and draw a dotted line across the tag board there. Then have them connect the dots with their rulers. T squares are especially helpful because the children can slide and anchor it across the top of the tag board. Model the following process on chart paper using the measurements of an average child in your class.

3. Remind the children that the tag board is 22 inches wide. Ask how far in they would need to measure to find the middle. Have children measure 11 inches into the tag board and mark the middle.

4. Ask two or three children to read the measurement of the length of their heads from forehead to chin. On your example use one of the measurements to show children how to measure the correct number of inches down from the first line drawn and mark that place and make a line there. Be sure to keep marking at the middle of the paper. Now have children use the measurement of the length of their heads and mark that place on their tagboard.

5. Talk about symmetry and the symmetry of the shapes of the children's heads. Then have them draw their head between the two lines at the center.

6. Continue modeling and having the children measure and draw the rest of their bodies using their homework sheets.

7. Once they're finished, the children can color and then cut themselves out. These self-portraits look great hung on windows, bulletin boards, or walls. (See page 62 for a writing integration.)

What about centimeters?

Continue along the same lines by having the children pretend they've shrunk. Tell them they're so small that they now need to measure themselves in centimeters. Have them pick a size like 10 to 30 centimeters. Then tell them to list and measure 10 things in the classroom in or on which they could fit.

(H) Repeat this activity for homework. (For a writing integration, see page 64.)

Assessment Tip

To assess your students' understanding of inches and centimeters, give them a list of things in the classroom of various sizes. Ask them to decide which ones they could more easily measure with centimeters, and which would be easier to measure with inches and feet. On a list that included tadpoles and the teacher. My students preferred the centimeters for the tadpoles and inches/feet for the teacher.

Hands-on and creative activities are effective for teaching math to second graders. Applying the skills this way encourages, extends, and enriches learning. Second graders are ready to work independently and cooperatively to effectively solve problems and augment the knowledge they've gained.

Teacher resources for teaching math

Barratta-Lorton, Mary. *Mathematics Their Way.* Addison-Wesley, 1976.

Brunetto, Carolyn Ford. *Math Art Projects and Activities.* Scholastic, 1997.

Burns, Marilyn. *About Teaching Mathematics: A K-8 Resource.* Heinemann, 1996.

Burns, Marilyn, and Bonnie Tank. *A Collection of Math Lessons, From Grades 1-3.* Heinemann, 1988.

Books about time

Clocks and More Clocks by Pat Hutchins. Macmillan, 1970.

8 O'clock by Jill Creighton. Scholastic, 1995.

The Grouchy Ladybug by Eric Carle. Harper Trophy, 1986.

Nine O'Clock Lullaby by Marilyn Singer. Harper Trophy, 1991.

Telling Time with Big Mama Cat by Dan Harper. Harcourt & Brace, 1998.

If you want to make a connection to the idea of parties and people arriving, try the following titles.

Books about parties

10 for Dinner by Jo Ellen Bogart. Scholastic, 1989.

The 329th Friend by Marjorie Weinman Sharmat. MacMillan, 1992.

Miss Spider's Tea Party by David Kirk. Scholastic, 1994.

Mouse's Birthday by Jane Yolen. G.P. Putnam, 1992.

Books to connect to Halloween

Haunted Tacos by Shannon Keegan. Scholastic, 1992.

The Hungry Thing Goes to a Restaurant by Jan Slepian and Ann Seidler. Scholastic, 1992.

Monster's Lunch Box by Marc Brown. Little Brown, 1995.

The Witches' Supermarket by Susan Meddaugh. Houghton Mifflin, 1991.

Additional children's literature for math

The April Rabbits by David Cleveland. Coward, McCann & Geoghegan, Inc., 1978.

Why Money Was Invented by Neal S. Godfrey. Silver Press, 1995.

My Little Sister Ate One Hare by Bill Grossman. Crown Publishers, 1996.

2x2=Boo! by Loreen Leedy. Holiday House, 1995.

Jelly Beans for Sale by Bruce Macmillan. Scholastic, 1996.

Bunches and Bunches of Bunnies by Louise Mathews. Dodd, Mead & Co., 1978.

17 Kings and 42 Elephants by Margaret Mahy. Penguin, 1987.

The Token Gift by Hugh William McKibbon. Annick Press, 1996.

One Hundred Is a Family by Pam Munoz Ryan. Hyperion Books for Young Children, 1994.

Math Curse by Jon Scieszka and Lane Smith. Penguin, 1995.

From One to One Hundred by Teri Sloat. Dutton, 1991.

Math Counts Length by Ruth Thomson, ed. Children's Press, 1995.

Shapes books

Color Zoo by Lois Ehlert. HarperCollins, 1989.

Grandfather Tang's Story by Ann Tompert. Crown Publishers, 1990.

Picture Pie 2 by Ed Emberly. Little, Brown & Co., 1996.

The Secret Birthday Message by Eric Carle. Harper Trophy, 1986.

The Shape of Things by Dayle Ann Dodds. Candlewick Press, 1994.

Thinkin' Things. Edmark Corp., 1993. (Computer Disk)

Measurement books

How Big Is a Foot? by Rolf Myller. Bantam Doubleday Dell Publishing Group Inc., 1990.

Inch by Inch by Leo Lionni. Astor House, 1960.

Is a Blue Whale the Biggest Thing There Is? by Robert E. Wells. Albert Whitman & Co., 1993.

Measuring Penny by Loreen Leedy. Henry Holt, 1997.

Game Map

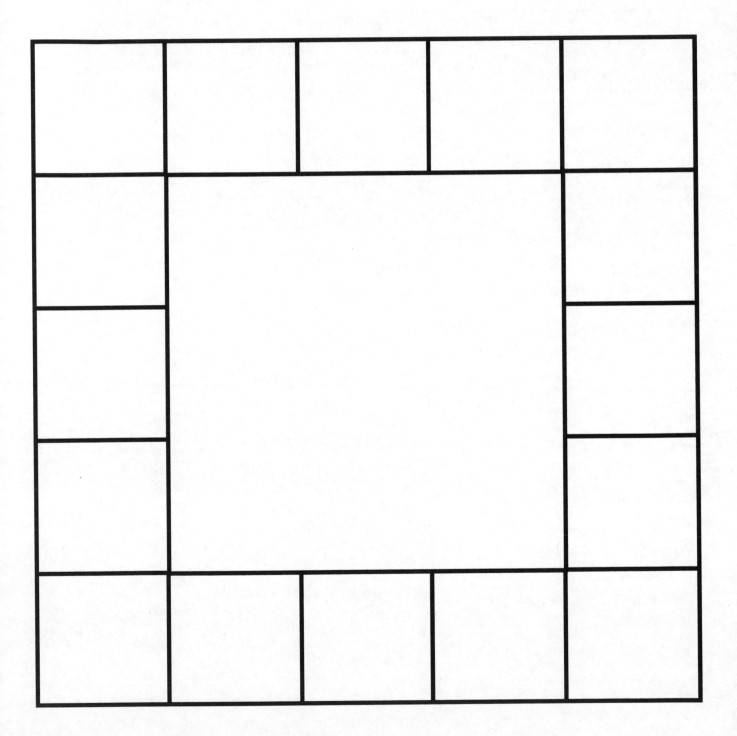

Game Paper

Write equations here.

Draw picture here.

Tesselation Patterns

Name_____ Date _____

Write the time on the lines. Include a.m. or p.m.
Draw hands on each clock.

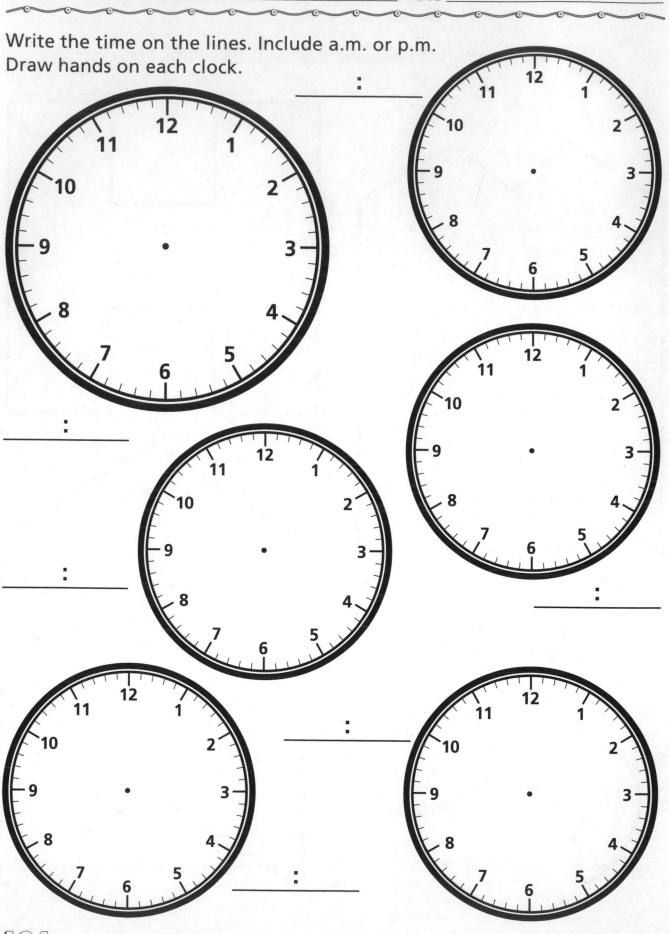

104

Bubble Templates

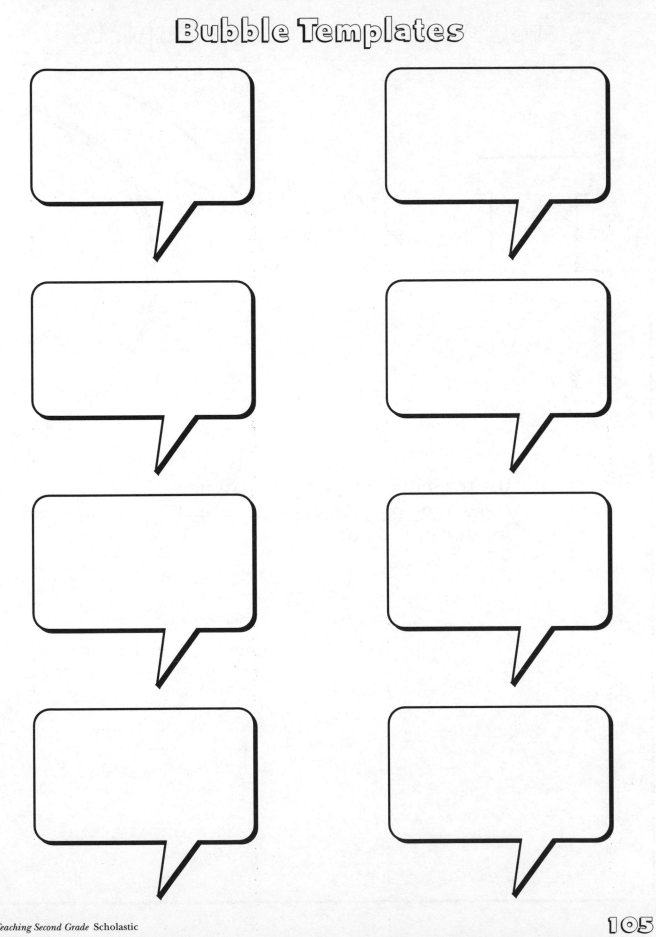

Creepy Café Building Template

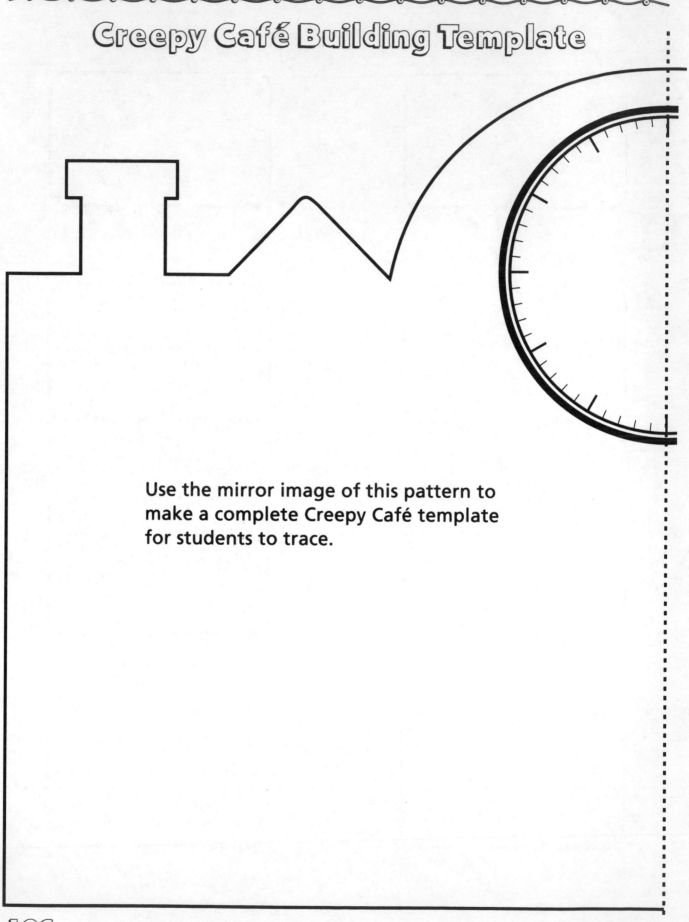

Use the mirror image of this pattern to
make a complete Creepy Café template
for students to trace.

Name_____ Date _____

Home Time

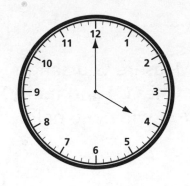

Find all the clocks and watches in your house. Write down **where** each one is, **what** each one is, and the time that is on it **when** you find it.

Room or Person	Watch or Clock	Time
Sample		
My room	clock	5:20 p.m.

_____

_____

_____

_____

_____

_____

_____

_____

_____

_____

_____

Measure Yourself!

Measure yourself in inches (") and feet ('). You will need help.

top of head to chin _____

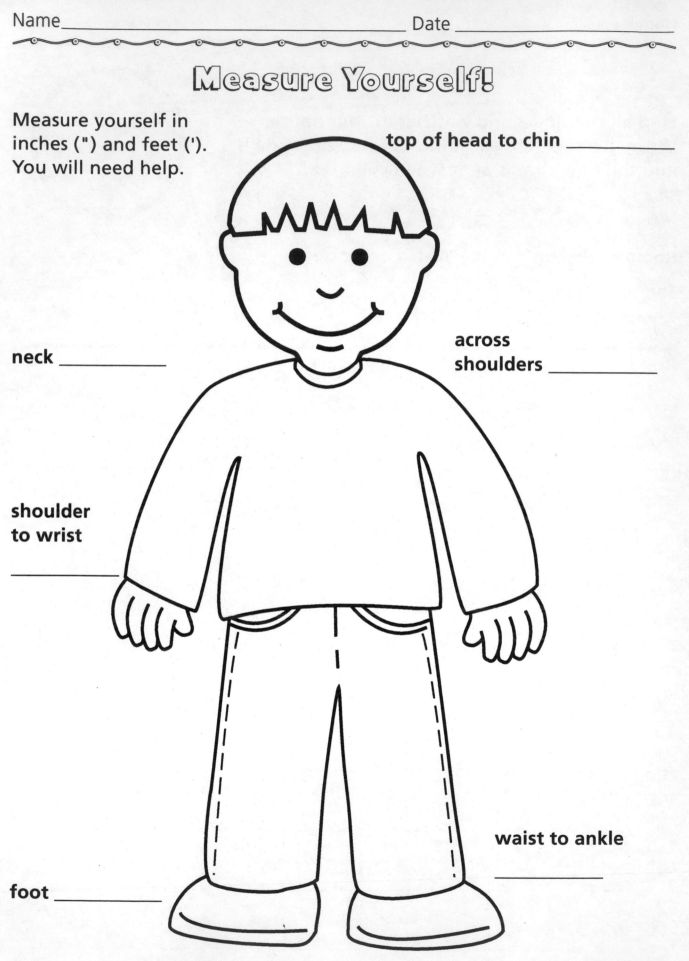

neck _____

across shoulders _____

shoulder to wrist

_____

waist to ankle

_____

foot _____

108

CHAPTER 8

Social Studies

Second graders are very interested in social studies concepts and enjoy personalizing these to their own lives. But don't be surprised that if you ask your young students where their family came from the answer is another local town. Still, now they're ready to go beyond self and family to consider more global concepts.

What do second graders know about social studies?

Some second graders may remember hearing the words. Hopefully, all have moved beyond the point of thinking the world revolves around them. Though they're still very fuzzy about time and change over time, they're ready to learn more about that. They're ready to consider maps, globes, and atlases because they can have more fun with them now that they can read.

What social studies concepts are appropriate for second graders?

First, check school, grade-level, district, and state curriculum. New York state's second-grade curriculum focuses on comparing the three kinds of communities—rural, suburban, and urban—beginning with the community in which students live. This works well for second graders.

What are good ways to teach social studies concepts?

If a district or school does not require a textbook, teaching with text sets— groups of books about the same subject—works well. Once you've gathered a set of books on a subject, you can work on related projects and activities. (See Chapter 11 for more information on text sets.)

Following is an example—using the rural, suburban, urban theme—of how to use text sets for social studies. Besides literature, the activities involve graphic organizers, large- and small-group reading experiences, a pop-up bulletin board, and individual student trifold books. You can transfer these activities to other topics by identifying the concepts you want to teach and fitting the activities to the subject at hand. For instance, you might use graphic organizers to compare regions like desert, rain forest, Arctic, and woodlands. The students can create pop-ups depicting each of these types of regions. They can write poetry about them.

Comparing Rural, Suburban, and Urban Communities

LESSON 1 **DISCUSSION AND LARGE-GROUP SHARED READING FOR POETRY AND GRAPHIC ORGANIZERS**
(Repeat this lesson for each of the three community types. This is done over a 3- to 4-week period. Allow about one week for each community type.)

MATERIALS

- 3 copies of the graphic organizer (page 117) for each child in your class, enlarged on 11" x 17" paper, then cut to 9" x 12"
- 1 copy of the graphic organizer on transparency for overhead projector or chart paper
- pencils, crayons, markers, chart paper, books
- 2 pieces 12"x 18" white construction paper for each child

*Note: As an alternative, just work on the overhead with your class and skip the individual copies for each child.

As you read books (see page 116 for a list of suggestions) to the class, be sure to discuss each in relationship to the concepts you're teaching. Have a map handy so that you can point out areas of the country in which these kinds of communities are established. Ask about other places children have visited. When children are going to travel, request that they send a postcard to school from wherever they go. Do the same over summer vacation. It's a good way to begin in fall.

1 Ask the children if they have ever heard the words *urban*, *suburban*, and *rural*. Continue the discussion with the type of community in which you live. Then help the children define the three types of communities briefly.

2 Read two or more books about one of the types of communities, stopping briefly to discuss concepts as you read. Compare books—and community types—using Venn diagrams.

3 After reading a book, write lists of words that describe the sights, sounds, feelings, and colors of that community on a chart.

ABIYOYO
A Giant
kids
the father and the son cause the problem
takes place in a Village
not wanted
the kid plays an instrument
boy does not have a name
father does not have a name

get rejected at the end they get liked
they both have problems
they Live in a Village
made a problem and solved it

There are no kids
sega caused the problem
they want the town to be the neighborhood
Same setting
makes the house of his dreams
main character Mr. Plumbean
no music

Big orange splot ↑

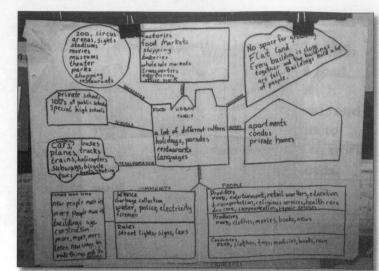

4 Display and hand out the graphic organizers. Label each with the three different community types. Work with the children to fill in the individual boxes. Have the children copy from yours so that spelling is correct. This and the reading can take at least two class periods.

5 Once each of the graphic organizers is completed in this way, make a trifold book.

Directions for trifold display

1. Fold each of the two pieces of construction paper in half.

2. Overlap one half of one piece of paper onto one half of the other piece of paper.

3. Glue these together so that you end up with three distinct sections for the trifold.

4. On the opposite side have the children draw urban, suburban, and rural scenes, respectively, to create their own display.

> **Assessment Tip**
> Children's drawings will help you easily determine how much knowledge of communities they have gained. For a verbal assessment, have children take turns sharing their trifold displays and discussing the differences.

LESSON 2   POP-UPS FOR BULLETIN BOARD

When children create a pop-up community bulletin board, they use what they've learned to make artistic and colorful comparisons. Vary each of the three community types by using different sized and different colored paper, and templates for houses, barns, and so on. (See pages 118–121.) You can vary the size of the paper and increase or reduce the size of the templates, depending on the size of your bulletin board. Be sure to scale accordingly. The sizes used here are those shown in the photo. Be sure to model for children how to create the pop-ups.

MATERIALS

For Urban pop-ups:
- building templates—short and tall
- 1 piece 9" x 12" gray construction paper for each child
- 1 piece 9" x 6" black paper construction paper for each child

To create the pop-up, have the children measure a fold line 2" along the 12" length of the gray paper, holding the paper vertically. Fold. Then measure 2" in from each side of paper. Mark and cut. Push in to create the pop-up ledge.

For Suburban pop-ups:
- house and short building templates
- 1 piece 9" x 12" green construction paper for each child
- 1 piece 5" x 8" white construction paper for each child

To create the pop-up, have the children measure a fold line 2" along the 9" length, holding paper horizontally. Fold. Then measure 3" in from each side of the paper. Mark and cut. Then push in to create the pop-up ledge.

For Rural pop-ups:
- barn, animal, corn, wheat, house, and short building templates
- 6" x 8" red, green, light brown construction paper
- 12" x 18" golden yellow or yellow construction paper

To create the pop-up, have the children measure a fold line 3" along the 18" length, holding the paper horizontally. Fold along that line. Then measure 4" in on each side for a cut line. Mark and cut. Push in to create the pop-up ledge.

General Directions for Pop-ups

Model and direct the children to measure where the pop-up ledge will go. Have the children trace, cut, and glue buildings and/or animals on, behind, and next to ledge to create a scene.

Note: Children may wish to place more in the scenes, including themselves, depending on the community in which you live.

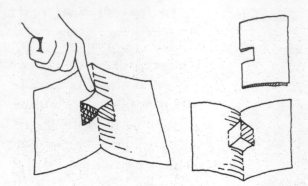

LESSON 3   POETRY WRITING

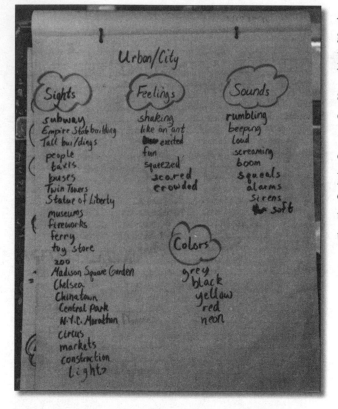

After the children to complete each of the graphic organizers and the corresponding pop-up. Take the time to have a related Writing Workshop. Use a chart to list sights, sounds, feeling, and colors related to each community.

Have the children use the chart to write comparison poems, pattern poems, rhyming poems, or listing poems for each of the communities. Plan to or have the children type these on the computer and display them on the pop-up bulletin board.

A sample comparison poem:

A city is as loud as a siren.

A city is as gray as an elephant.

A city is as big as all the tall buildings.

LESSON 4   SMALL-GROUP GUIDED READING

Small-group guided reading can reinforce the concepts you're teaching to the whole class, as well as link your reading lessons to the subject under study. Change over time is a difficult concept.

1 Read a set of books like *Little House*, *The Ox-Cart Man*, and *Roxaboxen*.

2 Have the children write about the changes and the causes of these changes.

Or for understanding the relationships in a community, try discussing and comparing the problems and solutions in *Coat of Many Colors*, *Abiyoyo*, and *The Big Orange Splot*.

3 Have the children read *It Takes a Village* and then make a Venn diagram with the class comparing your community to an African village.

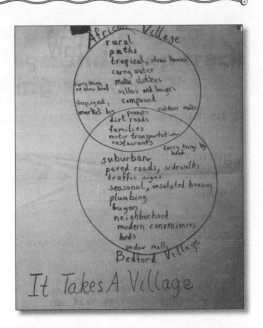

LESSON 5 MAPPING

Have maps of the local area, the United States, and the world available for viewing throughout the year. Whenever another state or country is mentioned, it's time to look at the map.

1 Using a local map, reproduce a graphic representation of the town in which you live. If it is a city, the major streets are enough.

2 Have the children make a representation of their home on a folded piece of paper. Approximating where they live, have them place their homes on the map.

3 Inside of the representation, have children write directions to their house.

H Send home a copy of the local map along with a request for parental help in writing these directions. (See page 122.) Go over the map in class first.

4 As a follow-up, look at the map again. Explain *latitude* and *longitude*. Locate points of interest. Number and letter graph paper to practice this concept.

Second graders extend their understanding of social studies concepts when they are immersed in learning. Reading, writing, and hands-on activities which help them interpret and transfer what they have learned enhance their discovery process.

Social studies resources for teachers

Fleming, Maria. *Homes.* Scholastic.

Hollenbeck, Kathleen. *Exploring Our World: Neighborhood and Communities.* Scholastic.

McCarthy, Tara. *Literature Based Geography Activities.* Scholastic.

Community books for large-group shared reading

Abuela by Arthur Dorros. Penguin, 1991.

Are We There Yet Daddy? by Virginia Walters. Viking, 1999.

The Cherry Tree by Daisaku Ikeda. Oxford University Press, 1990.

Citybook by Shelley Rotner and Ken Kreisler. Orchard Books, 1994.

Home Place by Crescent Dragonwagon. Macmillan, 1990.

House on Maple Street by Bonnie Pryor. William Morrow, 1987.

Me on the Map by Joan Sweeney. Crown Publishers, 1996.

My Place in Space by Robin and Sally Hirst. Orchard Books, 1988.

New York by Kathy Jakobsen. Little, Brown, 1993.

Ruby by Michael Emberly. Little, Brown, 1990.

Smoky Night by Eve Bunting. Harcourt Brace & Co., 1994.

Somewhere in Africa by Ingrid Mennen and Niki Daly. Penguin, 1990.

The Village of Round and Square Houses by Ann Grifalconi. Little Brown, 1986.

What a Wonderful World by George David Weiss and Bob Thiele. Simon & Schuster, 1995.

Whoever You Are by Mem Fox. Harcourt Brace & Co., 1997.

Community books for small-group reading

It Takes a Village by Jane Cowen-Fletcher. Scholastic, 1994.

Abiyoyo by Pete Seeger. Macmillan, 1986.

Big Orange Splot by D. Manus Pinkwater. Scholastic, 1990.

Coat of Many Colors by Dolly Parton. HarperCollins, 1994.

Little House by Virginia Lee Burton. Houghton Mifflin, 1942.

My Little Island by Frané Lessac. Macmillan, 1984.

Roxaboxen by Alice McLerran. William Morrow, 1991.

Community Graphic Organizer

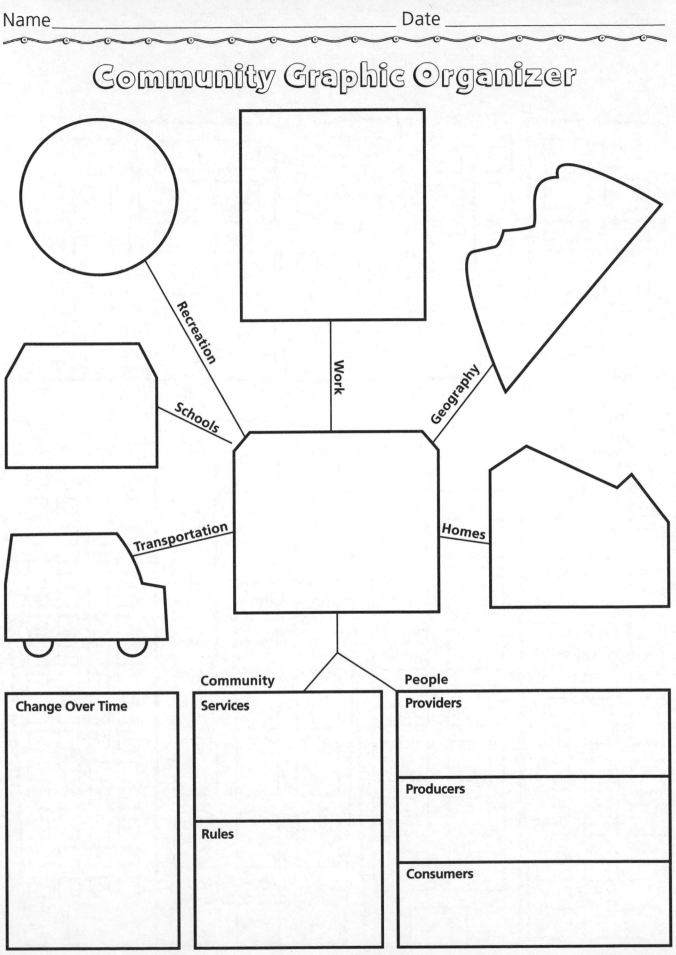

Recreation

Schools

Work

Geography

Transportation

Homes

Community

People

Change Over Time

Services

Providers

Rules

Producers

Consumers

Community Templates

Community Templates

Name_____ Date _____

Community Templates

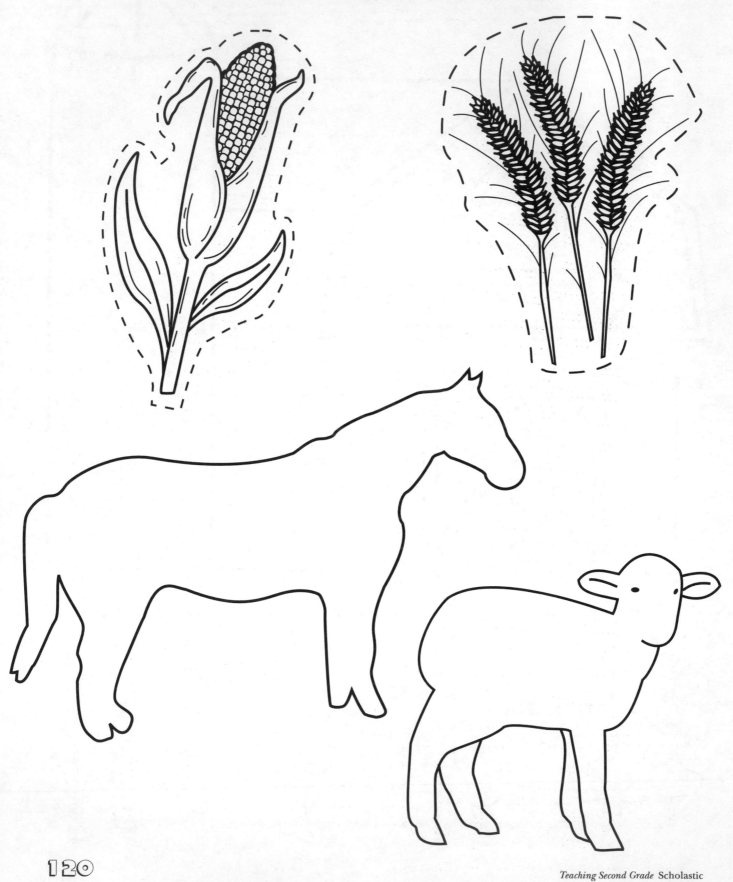

Teaching Second Grade Scholastic

Community Templates

From My House to School

Homework: Write directions to your house from school.

Return on _____.

Look at the map again with your parents. You just need to write general directions to get to your street. Please use the lines below. Write neatly, as always. You'll need to copy the information as part of a larger writing piece.

For instance, I would write:

_____

_____

_____

_____

_____

My address is

_____

Leaving our school,

_____

_____

_____

_____

I know my neighbors. They are

_____

My neighborhood is

_____

CHAPTER 9

Science

Second graders are fascinated by even the simplest experiments, and it's fun to do experiments with them. They can be trusted not to touch, and they're ready to sit, wait, and observe. They enjoy comparing outcomes and ideas. They love reading about, and looking at, pictures of real things.

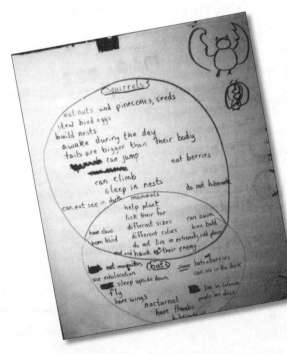

What do second graders know about science concepts?

Some second graders know that they like science. This may have much to do with watching the Discovery Channel and *The Magic School Bus*. Because they are developing writers, they're ready to experiment and even record some observations. When second graders hear the word *science*, their response is usually something having to do with plants and animals.

What are some effective ways to teach science?

First, check the district science curriculum. It can be enhanced with literature, but do not rely on trade books alone to teach the concepts. (See the list of teacher resources for science at the end of this chapter.)

For second graders, observations and simple experiments are best. You

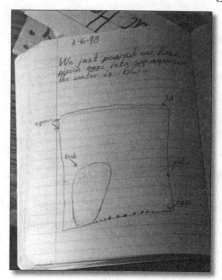

can have the children record their observations in one of several ways: keeping track of them in a journal specifically used for science; using a type of log for each set of experiments or observations; or noting them in their writing journals. Teach the children how to diagram (to illustrate what they see accurately and label with the correct vocabulary) using lines and arrows to point to specific parts of their drawing. (See photo at left.)

Text sets with activities and projects help children make science connections. Following is a text set with a science focus. The techniques, projects, and activities used in these lessons can be applied to other science studies. This approach is also a good way to begin teaching second graders about inquiry-based learning or research.

Comparing Squirrels to Bats

For this unit each child will create a fall picture made of cut paper that includes a Venn diagram comparing squirrels to bats. The unit works especially well in the fall because the leaves are changing, something that is familiar to the children. This grouping of activities incorporates text sets for squirrels, bats, and trees. (See page 130 for book suggestions.) The lessons can be done in large and small groups. Or you can use one text set that includes at least one book about squirrels, one about bats, and one about trees. With a large group, you'll read books to your class and gather facts on a chart with them. The fact gathering can also be done on a chart as you work with small groups. The approach you take may depend on the availability of books and the abilities within your class. (See Chapter 11 for general techniques for teaching with text sets.) Throughout the unit you can be reading books to the whole class to enhance the study.

MATERIALS

- 12" x 18" brown construction paper and blue construction paper (for tree trunk)
- 6" x 6" squares of yellow and red construction paper (for Venn diagram)
- 3" x 6" piece of orange construction paper (for overlapping part of Venn diagram)
- 4" x 4" pieces of various colors of construction paper (for leaves)
- tree, leaf, and Venn diagram templates (See pages 132–133.)
- scissors, glue
- directions on sentence strips (optional)
- black ink erasable pens
- crayons

LESSON 1   GETTING STARTED: LARGE-GROUP SHARED READING

1 Take a walk or look outside the window and get a discussion going about what's changing outside right now.

2 Read Betsy Maestro's book about trees, *Why do Leaves Change Colors?* (HarperCollins, 1994). Discuss what the children have learned from the book, bringing out major concepts such as cycles, seasons, and temperature.

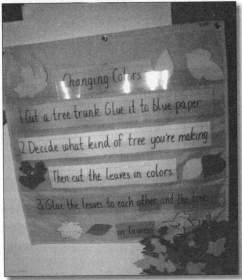

(H) For homework, have the children write an observation of a tree. Instruct them to observe a tree for five to ten minutes and describe what they see. The next day use a couple of the observations to instruct the class on descriptive writing and sentence structure.

3 Put the materials needed to create the fall picture at an Imagination Station center or set it up as a full-class project. Show the children how to trace the templates and cut and glue the pieces to create their picture.

LESSON 2   LARGE-GROUP SHARED READING

Read *Tree Trunk Traffic* by Bianca Lavies (Penguin, 1993) or another book about animals in trees. Reading this book can generate a discussion about how several animals live in, on, and under trees. Explain that over the next couple of weeks the class will be learning about two of these animals—squirrels and bats.

LESSON 3   BEGINNING THE INQUIRY

1 Remind children of what a KWL chart is. Then have them write on top of a page in their journals "What do I know about squirrels?" Give the class about 10 to 15 minutes to write independently.

2 Sit in a circle. Have each child share something he or she has written, asking them not to repeat something already said.

3 Once the children have had an opportunity to share, have them title another page in their journal "What would I like to know about squirrels?" Give the class about 10 to 15 minutes to complete this task. Then return to the circle and repeat step 2.

Proceeding from here will depend on whether you plan to use large group, or small group/individual reading.

LESSON 4   INTRODUCING FACT GATHERING

Large-group shared reading

1 Read *Nuts to You* by Lois Ehlert (Harcourt, Brace, Jovanovich, 1993).

2 Discuss how, though this is a fiction book, the author incorporated facts.

3 Show where the facts are in the back of the book. Read some and write three to five facts on a chart titled "What I Learned About Squirrels."

Small-group or individual reading

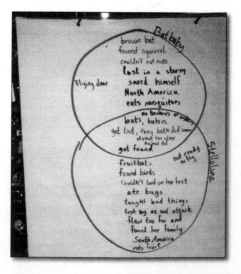

If there aren't enough books about squirrels and bats for the whole class, you can divide your class according to what *is* available. Some children can work on squirrels while others work on bats. Children can work in pairs or in groups of four, sharing the reading and gathering of facts. Facilitate this split of reading materials by helping the small groups or meeting with groups as they read the same book. If you're planning to split the class, it's important to do a large-group shared reading on bats, too. (See page 45 for more on flexible reading groups.)

1 Give each child (or group) a book about squirrels suitable for his or her (their) reading ability. Instruct the class to respond to their reading by writing three to five facts in their reading notebook on a page titled "Squirrel Facts." They can add to their facts each day as they read.

2 Meet and work with children, or groups of children, to check comprehension and encourage fact finding.

(H) For homework, have the children title a page in their writing journals "Squirrel Observation." Tell the children that they are to go home and observe a squirrel for five to ten minutes and write down their observations. Be sure to warn them not to get too close to the squirrel.

LESSON 5   INTRODUCING BATS

1 Read *Batbaby* by Robert Quackenbush (Random House, 1997) or *Stellaluna* by Jannell Cannon (Harcourt Brace, 1993.) Discuss the stories and whether they could really happen, or read both and compare the two with a Venn diagram.

2 Discuss what the author needed to know about bats.

3 Repeat the process as described in Lesson 4 with small groups reading bat books (see page 126).

LESSON 6   MAKING THE VENN DIAGRAM FOR EACH CHILD'S FALL PICTURE

1 Set up tables with the precut red, orange, and yellow paper; circle templates; glue; and scissors.

2 Tell the children they're going to prepare a cut-paper Venn diagram that will be glued to their tree. Have each child trace, cut, and glue together his or her tricolor Venn. Then they trace and cut the yellow circle, glue the orange ellipse in place, then hold these up to the light to check placement for the red circle.

3 Create a class Venn on a chart or on an overhead projector by drawing two intersecting circles, one in yellow and one in red. Then go over the intersection with an orange marker.

4 Have the children bring their reading notebooks to review and volunteer facts about each animal. Common facts go in the orange center, squirrel facts in the yellow section, and bat facts in the red section.

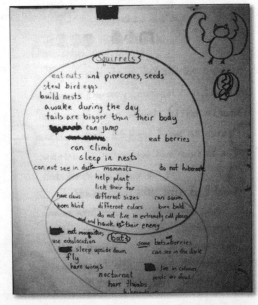

5 Once the full-class Venn is complete and the children's individual paper Venns are dry, have the children use erasable black ink pen to copy the class Venn onto their paper Venns, then glue these to their trees.

DRAWING A SQUIRREL AND A BAT FOR THE TREE

A mini drawing lesson is fun for the children and helps them hone their observation and visual discrimination skills.

1 Discuss with the children the shapes they can see when they look at pictures of squirrels and bats. What are the shapes of the heads, tails, eyes, ears, and so on?

2 Try to draw the animals yourself first. Then give the children time to draw theirs.

3 Have the children draw some squirrels or bats for a squirrel-and-bat Poetry Place display. (See photos and poems below.) Then have them glue some to their fall pictures. The fall pictures are now complete and ready for display.

2+2+2+2+2 Squirrels
by Valerie SchifferDanoff

Ten little squirrels sat in a tree
The first two said,
"Look at what we see!"
The next two said,
"Children having fun!"
The next two said,
"We should really run!"
The next two said,
"Let's hide in the shade."
The next two said,
"Why we're not afraid."
But away they did run.
And then there were none.

Assessment Tip
Assess these lessons by having children write in their journals, "What I learned about squirrels and bats." Then have them discuss and share their knowledge.

Whisky, Frisky

Whisky, frisky, hippity-hop
Up he goes, to the treetop!
Whirly, twirly round and round
Down he scampers, to the ground.
Furly, curly, what a tail.
Tall as a feather, broad as a sail.
Where is his supper? In the shell.
Snappity, crackity, out it fell.

Little Squirrel
by Ethel Hopper

A little squirrel runs up and down
In our old walnut tree.
All day he carries nuts away,
As busy as can be.
Mother says he stores them safe
For food when north winds blow;
I wonder how the squirrel knows
That some day there'll be snow.

What are some possibilities for using live animals in the classroom?

Not being fond of keeping caged animals, this question is difficult for me to answer. However, if you want to use a live animal, go for one that's easy to care for and won't bite. Raising frogs is a possibility. Frogs require an aquarium, distilled or treated water, and patience. The children are quite fascinated by observing the eggs-to-tadpoles-to-frogs cycle. It takes about 12 weeks. Contact Carolina Biological Supplies, 800-334-5551, for these and other live animal possibilities.

> ### Assessment Tip
> Assess by having the children make a small model of the animal's habitat using a triarama or diorama. Give the children paper on which to "map" their display before they begin. Then have them create it using tag board or a shoe box and plasticine clay to create their animals. Have the children each present their displays to the class and discuss what they've included.

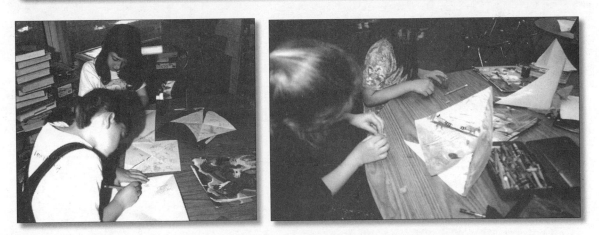

How about experiments and learning centers?

Second graders love experiments. They are ready to observe and record results, too. (See page 165 for an experiment on yeast.) They are also ready to help set up learning centers and be responsible for keeping them in order. You can make these centers available for a couple of hours, a day, or a week.

Water Museum

You might turn the classroom into a museum for a day. A water museum is easy because water is plentiful and most of the items you'll need are readily available. Make the children responsible for bringing in things that combine, or don't combine, with water (from whipped cream to food coloring), things that float in water (bath toys, corks), things that are powered by water (water toys), things that water flows through (hoses, water toys), things that repel water (raincoats, umbrellas, plastic drop cloths). (See a sample checklist you can send home with the children on page 134.)

Brainstorm the lists with the children, and be sure everyone is responsible for bringing something on the chosen day. Plastic drop cloths are a must for an indoor museum or an outside area if weather permits.

When you're planning your Water Museum, begin with a KWL chart. Set up the museum in the morning so children can complete the chart in the afternoon while the experience is still fresh in their minds.

Second graders are still at an age where they are amazed by simple things. Yet they are quite capable of theorizing, observing, experimenting, recording, gathering information, and drawing conclusions.

Science references for teachers

Goldish, Meish. *101 Poems & Songs for Young Learners.* Scholastic, 1996.

Kepler, Lynne. *Windowsill Science Centers.* Scholastic, 1996.

Kepler, Lynne *A Year of Hands-on Science.* Scholastic, 1996.

Olien, Rebecca. *Exploring Plants.* Scholastic, 1997.

Schecter, Deborah. *Science Art.* Scholastic, 1997.

Books about trees, squirrels, and bats

Batbaby by Robert Quackenbush. Random House, 1997.

Bats by Gail Gibbons. Holiday House, 1996.

Bats by Cindy Kendall. Dial, 1995.

The Bat in the Dining Room by Crescent Dragonwagon. Marshall Cavendish Corp, 1997.

Bats and Other Animals of the Night by Joyce Milton. Random House, 1994.

Bats Night Fliers by Betsy Maestro. Scholastic, 1994.

Busy, Busy Squirrels by Colleen Stanley Bare. Dutton, 1991.

The Cherry Tree by Daisaku Ikeda. Alfred A. Knopf, 1991.

The Elephant's Wrestling Match by Judy Sierra. Penguin, 1992.

Flying Squirrel at Acorn Place by Barbara Gaines. Soundprints Corp. Audio, 1998.

Gray Squirrel by Christine Butterworth. Steck-Vaughn/Macmillan, 1988.

The Great Ball Game: A Muskogee Story retold by Joseph Bruchac. Penguin, 1994.

A Log's Life by Wendy Pfeffer. Simon & Schuster, 1997.

Loose Tooth by Steven Kroll. Holiday House, 1984.

The Magic School Bus Going Batty by Joanne Cole. Scholastic, 1996.

Nuts to You! by Lois Ehlert. Harcourt Brace Jovanovich, 1993.

Once There Was Tree by Natalia Romanova. Penguin, 1985.

Red Leaf, Yellow Leaf by Lois Ehlert. Harcourt Brace Jovanovich, 1991.

Red Squirrel by Christine Butterworth. Steck-Vaughn/Macmillan, 1988.

Sarah Squirrel and the Lost Acorns by Julie Sykes. Little Tiger Press, 1996.

The Squirrel by Margaret Lane. Penguin, 1981.

Stellaluna by Janell Cannon. Harcourt Brace,1993.

Tree Trunk Traffic by Bianca Lavies. Penguin, 1993.

The Tree that Would Not Die by Ellen Levine. Scholastic, 1995.

The Tree by Gallimard Jeunesse and Pascale de Bourgoing. Scholastic, 1992.

Why Do Leaves Change Colors? by Betsy Maestro. HarperCollins, 1994.

World's Weirdest Bats by M. L. Roberts. Troll, 1996.

Zipping, Zapping, Zooming Bats by Ann Earle. HarperCollins, 1995.

Tree Templates

Venn Diagram
Template

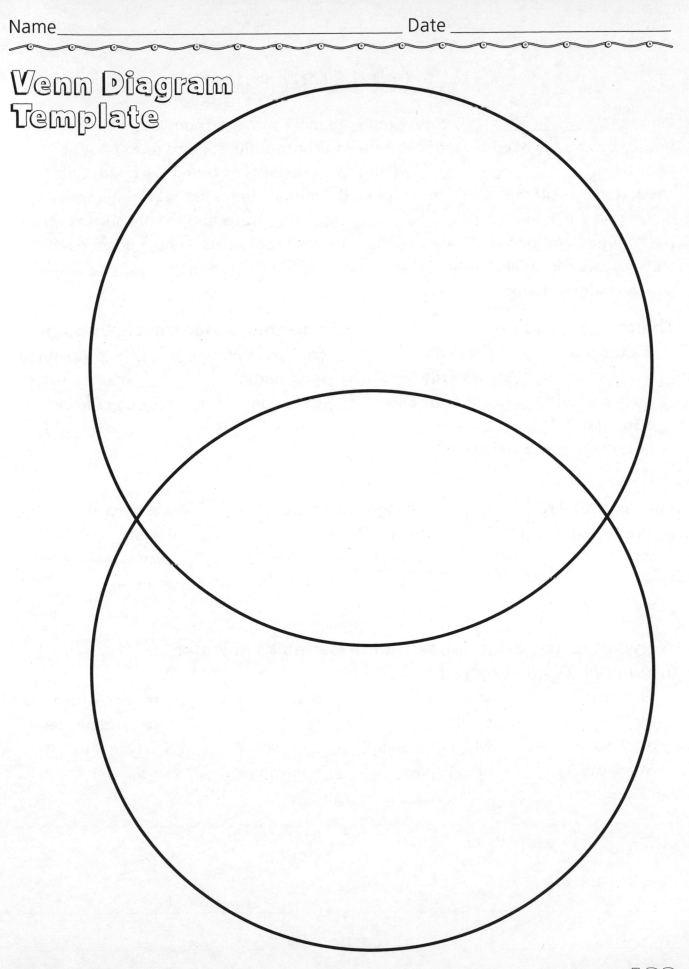

Water Museum

On _____, we are going to make our classroom into a Water Museum. To do this we need everybody's help and contributions. Items must be sent in no later than _____. Below are checklists of things we need. Only check it in one place if the item is repeated. Reusable items like watering cans and water toys will be returned by _____. Disposable items such as toothpaste, sugar, and cinnamon are to be sent in small containers. Send only an ounce in a disposable container. Write yourself a reminder. Cut along the dotted line and keep the reminder at home.

Things that hold water

__bucket   __squeeze bottle
__bin   __spray bottle
__watering can   __small kiddie pool
__water gun   __baby bathtub
__water bottle   __disposable
                        containers

Things that water travels through

__small piece of hose   __fire hydrant toy
__spray bottle   __small sprinkler
__water gun   __dog shower
__water wheel

Things that are powered by water

__sprinkler
__water wheel
__water toy

Things that travel by water

__boats
__balls
__ducks

Waterproof things

__plastic drop cloth
__raincoat

We want to see what happens to these things in water.
Bring only a small amount.

__toothpaste   __soap   __shampoo   __shaving cream
__food coloring   __conditioner   __cooking oil   __salt and pepper
__perfume   __whipped cream __chocolate   __mayonnaise
__cream cheese   __orange juice   __cinnamon   __baking soda
__Alka Seltzer   __other _____

Reminder

I need to bring

_____

_____to school by _____.

CHAPTER 10

Writing a Daily Letter

During my eight years as a first-grade teacher, I wrote a letter to my class every day. As I moved up to second grade, I continued the practice. Integrating second-grade skills and content added a new dimension to the medium. In order to encourage the children to keep a personal journal, I present the daily letter as my personal journal. After all, a personal journal can be written to yourself or to someone else.

What is a daily letter?

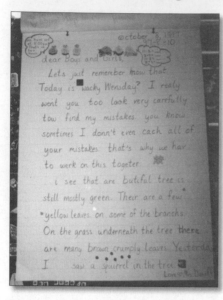

My daily letter is a friendly letter I write to my class on chart paper. It can introduce and reinforce skills and concepts, but keeping the format friendly is the key to success. The daily letter can serve as a model every day. It can include word play, spelling words, vocabulary words, and so on. It's easy to include these when you're writing to the class about things you're thinking about—activities, the weather, the weekend, ideas to share, and so on. Think of it as writing to a friend, or a whole class of friends. Every day I send my daily letter home with the helper of the day. Each child in the class receives the letter about once a month. This keeps parents up to date on what's happening in the class because it mentions the themes, curriculum, and skills I'm teaching.

What are some tips for practicing and writing a daily letter?

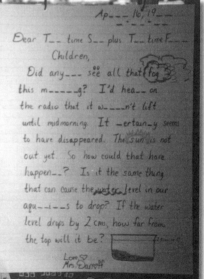

Try some sample letters at home and then copy them onto chart paper. I write the letter in the morning before school begins. It allows me to include weather changes and other up-to-the-minute events. Try not to write predictions of what will happen that day. You'll avoid disappointing the children if something you predicted doesn't happen. Most important, relax. Think about the purpose for writing, why you're teaching, what you love about being around children. Writing to second graders is easier than writing to first graders. They can read. Writing the daily letter should be natural, similar to the way you speak or would write to a friend. Remember, this is a model for the children for writing, handwriting, and more.

What might be included in the daily letter?

Include the date, salutation, body, and closing. Eight to ten sentences is the average length. You might include a daily math problem for the class to solve, the day's schedule or special events, weather discussions, activity discussions, theme discussions, questions to the class.

How long does it take to read the daily letter with the class?

There's more to that question than meets the eye. By incorporating suggested activities (see below), the daily letter becomes a learning experience. For instance, by omitting letters in words, the cloze procedure and spelling skills are incorporated. It could take 20 to 45 minutes to read, and discuss, the daily letter.

What activities might a basic daily-letter lesson include?

1. Children reading independently.
2. Choral reading or individual children reading sentences.
3. Children answering comprehension questions based on content.
4. The helper of the day coming up and filling in the empty spaces for the day's date.
5. Children taking turns completing words, peers coaching one another, and the whole class spelling the words together as each child writes.
6. Discussing concepts and ideas.

A list of lesson and activity ideas is found on page 138.

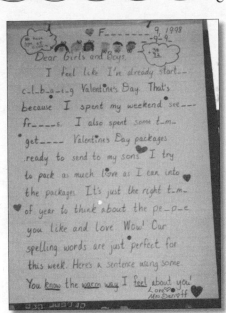

Lessons and Activities to Use with a Daily Letter

- Omit letters in words for cloze.

- Clap words for auditory discrimination and for teaching syllables.

- Circle punctuation and sentences with highlighter.

- Have the children rhyme words with a word used in the letter. Write these in the margin of the letter or keep separate reference charts for rhymed words.

- Write riddles about spelling words.

- Give word choices using homonyms. Have children circle the correct ones.

- Write antonyms. Have the children write the correct words.

- Once a week write a letter with spelling and/or punctuation errors. Begin with 5 obvious ones and gradually work up to a maximum of 20 errors. Have the children be the editors.

- Change the salutation.

- Incorporate story problems for math.

- Work on similes.

- Refer children to the letter to find words they'd like to spell correctly.

- Circle verbs, nouns, adjectives.

- Incorporate descriptive language and cite these for a mini-lesson before journal writing.

- Circle suffixes and root words.

The daily letter can be multifaceted. It provides the teacher and the children with opportunities for exchanging ideas within a personal context that changes daily.

CHAPTER 11

Teaching with Text Sets

Searching for, collecting, and using a group of books
that enhance the curriculum can be an exciting way to
teach. Solid, related groupings of books and other
texts provide rich resources for the teacher and the class.

What is a text?

A text is something written (books, articles, poems) or otherwise presented (dance, gesture, video, photography) that is a source of meaningful communication.

What is a text set?

A text set is an arrangement or grouping of texts that encourages students to make connections. The teacher can support this exciting way of learning by gathering texts that are conflicting—present different views; complementary—present varied and repeated aspects of a subject; controlling—one text is used to frame the reading of other texts; synoptic—present different versions of the story or event (from different cultures, for example); or dialogic—characters, people, themes, and events appear and reappear across many texts. (See bibliography for article from Teacher's Desk Reference/Scholastic Literacy Place by Douglas K. Hartman).

Why teach with text sets?

Text sets encourage children to make the connections inside school that they make naturally outside of school. For instance, my sons, who at ages eight and ten loved to play baseball, also loved collecting and reading baseball cards. They liked going to baseball games and watching games on television. They wanted to see baseball-themed movies and, best of all, read baseball-themed books. They read fiction, nonfiction, history, and biographies related to baseball. Similarly, at school, instead of reading just one book and having one discussion about a subject, a set of books or texts can help students make connections. With the world's communication growing through the electronic media and the global community, we all need to learn to connect relevant aspects of the information that surrounds us.

What are some tips for gathering sets of texts?

Once you get started you'll be surprised to see how easy it is to create text sets. Basically, you begin by choosing a subject. Sometimes a favorite book, topic in the news, or experience will stimulate the choice. Next, look up the subject in the library or in catalogs, and you'll find other books and activities to support your topic. Amazon.com on the Internet is a fabulous source. Spend time reviewing the books to decide whether or not they're appropriate. Another great way to gather texts is to ask the children if they have anything at home to contribute. Books, videos, postcards, games, figurines, toys, photographs, music, and even guest speakers, are things my students have brought in.

What are some ways to help students make connections?

It's most important to ask questions that require or prompt students to consider more than one text in their answer. Comparing texts and their presentation of the same subject (for example, through a Venn diagram), and discussing the variants, is a good way to show students different approaches to the same subject. You can also start with a KWL, having students consider what they know, what they want to know, and then what they have learned. Presenting activities that build relationships among the texts also provides connections. Finally, allow children to make their own connections by asking what they'd like to find out more about in a text. For example, if they're reading *Goldilocks and the Three Bears*, they might like to know more about real bears, read other versions, or put on a play. Extend the KWL chart by adding another W for where can we find out?

Is there one key thing to remember if you're using text sets?

Yes. Don't overload, stretch, or push a subject beyond reasonable boundaries. It's easy to get carried away. If one intriguing thing you're eager to use doesn't connect naturally, write it down and save it in a special file for another time. Use your judgment.

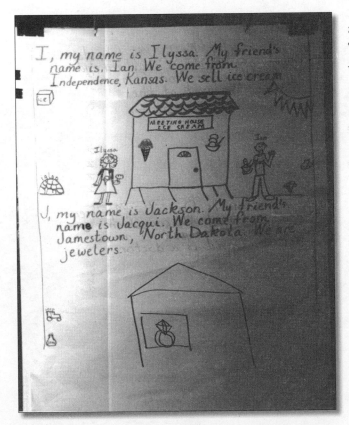

Following are two text sets and related activities that have been successful for me. The first, FLIP OVER GROWING, is a great way to start the school year. You can do the second, A–Z U.S.A. COMMUNITIES, anytime, but it's just right for establishing your expectations for writing mechanics, assessing reading, and helping children begin to understand communities. (There are also text sets listings in Chapters 5, 7, 8, 9, and 12.) Book suggestions for the text sets presented in this chapter are found on page 151.

Flip Over Growing

The focus of this text-set unit is understanding growing and how it affects change over time. Second graders are ready to understand that they are getting older and that their role in family and community is changing. To learn about these concepts, the children create a flip book that shows how they've grown and changed. They'll see that their growth enables, and will continue to enable, them to take part in more activities and responsibilities.

MATERIALS

- drawing paper cut to 9" x 4" or 9"x 8" folded in half to make it 9" x 4"
- white tag board cut to 9" x 4"
- colored pencils
- scissors
- T square or ruler

Directions for Making the Flip Book

A flip book is bound in the center and pages are cut into sections so that different sections can flip at different times or together. Prepare a flip book for each of your students in advance of the lessons. If a binding machine is available, you'll bind eight pieces of 9" x 4" paper to make a book for each child. If binders are not available, you can use a long-arm stapler to attach the pages.

Fold five pieces of 9" x 8" paper in half so that it's a 9" x 4" booklet when stapled in the middle. Staple the pages together in the middle along the fold. Be sure that a slight margin of space is left to hold the book together when the pages are being cut into sections.

Make a model book. It can be about you.

LESSON 1   LARGE-GROUP SHARED READING

Read the book *New Shoes for Silvia* by Johanna Hurwitz (William Morrow, 1993) or any of the other suggested books. Generate a discussion about the fact that children grow until about the age of 18 and about ways we can tell we're growing. Discuss how they lose their baby teeth, that their hair and feet grow, and that they need progressively larger-sized clothes. Share your teacher-made flip book and tell your class they'll be making a flip book about themselves as they learn about how growing affects changes in them and things they can do.

(H) Send home the I am Growing reproducible on page 152. The children may need their parents' help to remember being one, two, three, and so on. The send-home goes up to age six, since second graders are turning either seven or eight.

Each day before working on the books, read another story and discuss the changes taking place.

LESSON 2   PREPARING THE FLIP BOOKS BY MEASURING

1. Hand out rulers (or preferably T squares) and flip books.

2. Discuss that the ruler has 12 inches, which equals 1 foot. Point out numbers and delineations. Briefly discuss the millimeter side of the ruler and tell the children that they may use that at another time. If you're using centimeters, adjust the size of book accordingly so that it can be divided into three equal parts.

3. Discuss the parts of the book—the cover, the pages, and the back cover. Turn to the first page.

4. Show the children how to use a T square by holding one on an edge to make it steady. Or discuss holding a ruler straight. Have the children place the bottom edge of their ruler on the bottom edge of the paper and gently draw a line across the page. Explain that this is the line they'll write on.

5. Have children measure the book. Ask if anyone knows how to divide it into three equal parts. Show them how to mark a line at 3" intervals to divide the 9" length of the page into equal parts.

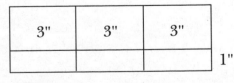

6. Have the children turn their rulers around to draw the vertical lines that divide the one page into three pages. Have them make sure these lines intersect the interval marks and the writing line.

7. Continue until all pages are divided.

WRITING AND ILLUSTRATING

This should take three to four 45-minute writing periods.

1 Have the children use their filled-out I Am Growing homework sheets to write on the lines for the pages for each year. When I was one/ I could .../ I wanted to ...

   When they get to their current age, they'll change the words to:
   Now I am/ I can.../ I want to...
   If they are a writing about their next birthday, they can write:
   When I am eight / I hope I can.../ I'd like to...

2 Once the writing is completed, have the children go through the book.

3 For the cover, brainstorm on a chart possible names for the book, such as: I Am Growing, My First Eight Years, I'm Flipping Over Growing.

4 Discuss cover design, and have the children write and illustrate their covers.

5 Have children carefully cut along lines drawn and watch the excitement as they flip over their flip books!

A-Z U.S.A. Communities

This text-set activity gives each child a first opportunity to write and publish a book. The whole class writes together. Then each child copies the book (personalizing when possible) into his or her individual book. The theme of A-Z U.S.A. Communities introduces the social studies concept of communities and helps children understand that there are communities all over the U.S. It also provides lots of writing-skills practice. The writing experience is based on the childhood poem *A, My Name Is Alice.* I suggest starting by having a copy of the book *A, My Name Is Alice* by Jane Baye (Penguin, 1984) or *A, My Name Is...* by Alice Lyne (Whispering Coyote Press, 1997) available. A great variety of alphabet stories at a wide range of fluency levels and about numerous subjects can help assess your students' interests and reading skills. (See page 43 for more on assessing reading, and page 42 for more on teaching reading.) This activity is a comfortable place to start the school year for you and your students.

Rewriting a class version of *A, My Name Is Alice* or *A, My Name Is...* is a fun way to introduce the alphabet-story genre. As a first full-class writing experience, it can incorporate mini-lessons for Writing Workshops.

(H) For a homework assignment, have children look in the local phone book to find services and businesses for each letter of the alphabet.

Explain to children that communities throughout the United States and around the world have differences and similarities. The families that make up each community bring their traditions and needs. They provide services and products, too.

On page 150 is the basic story my students and I wrote. You can change it by using the names of the children in your class and then simply referring to a United States atlas. Incorporate your own town and state names. Introduce this story with the following verse. I also have them copy it on the first page of their book.

> In U.S.A. communities,
> There are some similarities.
> People, places, sites, all things
> Families living there bring.
> Here's the story from A to Z,
> Of twenty-six communities.

MATERIALS

- ◎ alphabet stories
- ◎ white tag board cut into 10" squares, 2 per child
- ◎ white drawing paper cut into 10" squares, 10 per child
- ◎ a 14" ribbon for each child
- ◎ filament tape
- ◎ two-hole punch
- ◎ lined writing paper
- ◎ pencils and colored pencils
- ◎ 1 copy of a United States map for each child (See page 153.)

*optional: 26 pieces of colored tag board to make an alphabet frieze of the states or community places, e.g., firehouse, courthouse, school, and so on.

Directions for Setting Up an A-Z U.S.A. Book for Each Child

1 Cut 1" from the sides of one of the pieces of tag board. Then tape it back together with filament tape to create a hinge.

2 Place this on top of the 10" x 10" squares of drawing paper and the other piece of tag board to create covers and pages.

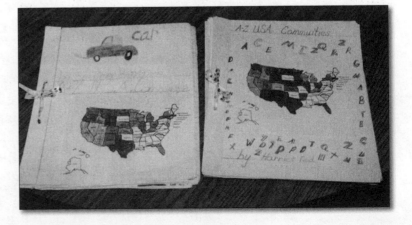

3 Use the 2-hole punch to punch through all the pages and covers.

4 Thread the ribbon through the holes and loosely tie the book together so the pages can be turned and folded back following the fold made by the filament-taped hinge.

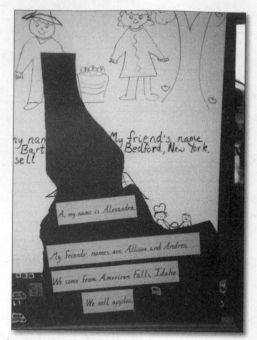

If you want to make an alphabet frieze of the class story, use an overhead projector and a map of the U.S. to trace the states onto tag board. Then write the words of the story on sentence strips and glue them to the appropriate state. In lieu of an overhead projector, cut tag to uniform size, glue a picture of each state onto the tag board and finish with the words on sentence strips. You'll find maps on various computer programs. Claris 4.0 has state maps in its library that can be enlarged. Or trace and copy maps from an atlas.

LESSON 1 GETTING STARTED WITH LARGE-GROUP SHARED READING

Gather a variety of alphabet stories from the library.

(H) Ask the children to bring alphabet story books from home.

This can be coordinated with the book review activity "Read All About It!" described in Chapter 2 (page 26).

1 Ask the class to recite the alphabet song.

2 Read an alphabet story to the children.

3 Continue reading alphabet stories to the class over the course of this project.

LESSON 2 INDIVIDUAL, PAIRED, AND SMALL-GROUP READING

Having more than one copy of the same book is great for paired or small-group reading. If you have only one copy of each book, then individualized reading also works. When ordering books for your classroom, consider ordering multiple copies of an alphabet story. Alphabet books are very approachable and are available in a wide range of fluency levels. For example, *Chicka Chicka Boom Boom* by Bill Martin (Simon & Schuster, 1989) is right for the beginning reader, *Alligator Arrived with Apples* by Crescent Dragonwagon (Aladdin, 1992) is perfect for the early fluent reader, and *A Is for Africa* by Ifeoma Onyeflulu (Penguin, 1993) can easily be read by the fluent reader. Children are comfortable picking up an alphabet book and reading it independently, which is an important habit to begin establishing in second grade.

1 Show the class your collection of alphabet books.

2 Tell them that after everyone has had an opportunity to read one or more of the stories, you're going to sort the books by type. Does the book tell a story as does *The ABC Mystery* by Doug Cushman (HarperCollins, 1993)? Does it list an item or items for each letter as does *Eating the Alphabet* by Lois Ehlert (Harcourt Brace Jovanovich, 1989)? Is it about one subject as is *The Icky Bug Book* by Jerry Pallotta (Charlesbridge, 1986)? After the children have read for about 25 minutes, call them together in a group and sort the books. Let the children know that you'll be studying alphabet books over the next two to three weeks and that they'll have lots of opportunities to read the stories.

3 Over the next two weeks, as the children read the alphabet stories, have them write responses in their reading journals. (See suggestions for reading responses on page 49.)

LESSON 3   SOCIAL STUDIES/ GEOGRAPHY

Before teaching the writing part of the activity, discuss the subject of the story.

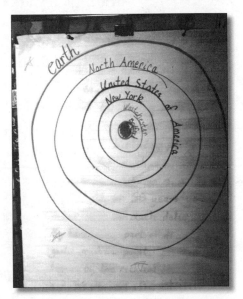

1 Show a globe and a United States map or atlas. Talk generally with the children about the earth and maps, explaining that the earth has six continents; that the United States is in North America; that the United States is made up of states; and that states have cities and towns. Point out your location on the map. To illustrate the relationships among places, draw concentric circles on a chart. Label the circles. (See photo.)

2 Explain that your town will be one of the communities in the story, though it may not be the first one. For example, our town is Bedford, New York, whose first letter is B, which is the second letter in the alphabet and in the story.

3 Before the children begin writing, point out the community and the state it is in on the map. Also discuss north, south, east, and west with children.

LESSON 4   WRITING AN A-Z STORY

Each writing session can incorporate a Writing Workshop mini-lesson focusing on various techniques and language mechanics as exemplified in the story you read. These lessons might be about sentence structure, proper nouns, writing styles, creative illustrations appropriate to the story, writing about what you know by using family/friends' names, and so on.

1 Show the children how to set up the format for each page of their book by modeling writing the first two letters (*A* and *B*) on chart paper. First draw a red margin line. Then write each letter's sentence and count down the correct number of lines you need (13 on the average $8\frac{1}{2}$" x $10\frac{1}{2}$" piece of paper) to fit two letters with their illustrations on a page.

2 Explain to the children that they are writing a class A-Z based on the poem "A, My Name Is….." Read the lines together. Review the format of the page. Direct the class' attention to the language mechanics, the punctuation, the use of the possessives and the plurals, proper nouns, and so on. Remind them of these by asking questions about them each time you write. By the fifth or sixth time you can omit some punctuation or letters and have the children tell you what should go where.

3 Hand out the lined writing paper, and explain to the children that they need to copy carefully, in their best handwriting, because there will be no rough draft. (They are going to paste these copies into their own individual books.) Have each child copy the first letter. Then count down the correct number of lines together. Have the children copy the second letter. Check their papers and have them illustrate these two letters. By the fourth or fifth letter the children can copy independently at their own pace, but be sure to check their writing as they go. Stress neatness and encourage creative illustrations.

4 While the children are writing, encourage those who are able to change words to personalize their own book. Have an atlas available.

5 Have the children store their finished pages in their writing folders until it's time to publish.

LESSONS 5 TO 7
PUBLISHING THE A-Z U.S.A. BOOKS

1 Show the children a typical title page. Have them make a rough copy of a title page in their books.

(H) This can be for homework the night before. (See the send-home sheet on page 153.)

2 Hand out the ribbon-bound books and have the children copy their title page. Using T squares for spacing is helpful.

3 The first leaf of the book is the title page, so skip that page. Then have the children glue the first page of the story and continue carefully using front and back pages until all the composition pages are glued inside the bound book. Caution the children not to skip pages as they glue and to use glue sparingly. Check for this as they go along.

4. Look at the book covers and discuss possible designs. Tell the children that you expect them to incorporate a map of the U.S.A. in their designs. You may want to hand out the maps (two for each child—one for the rough draft and one for the final cover) at this point so they can allow for spacing. Have the children make rough drafts of their cover designs. Ⓗ This might be done as homework.

5. Have the children copy the rough draft of their cover onto the final cover.

6. Have children glue their U.S.A. map to the cover. Then, using an overhead projector or pull-down map, have them read over their stories and color in each state used in the story.

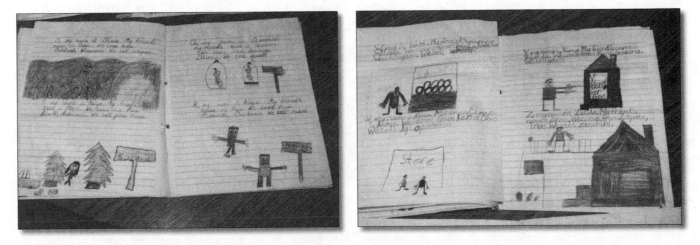

Celebration

A great way to celebrate the effort of the past few weeks is to have an A–Z party. On a chart, brainstorm a food for each letter of the alphabet. Assign each food to a child in you class. Finally, designate a day for them to bring in the food and enjoy an alphabet party!

A-Z U.S.A. Communities Poem

A, my name is Alexandra. My friend's name is Andrés. We come from American Falls, Idaho. We sell apples. (Or, I am an attorney and Andres works at the airport.)

B, my name is Beth. My friend's name is Brad. We come from Bedford, New York. We sell books. (Or, I work at a bank and Brad is a baker at the bakery.)

C, my name is Carl. My friend's name is Charlie. We come from Clearwater, Florida. We sell candles. (Or, we work in the courthouse.)

D, my name is Dana. My friend's name is Dave. We come from Deer Lodge, Montana. We sell daisies. (We own a dairy farm, or I am a dentist and Dave is a doctor.)

E, my name is Emily. My friend's name is Ed. We come from Eureka, Nevada. We sell eggs. (Or, I am an editor.)

F, my name is Fran. My friend's name is Fred. We come from Forest Grove, Oregon. We sell fish. (Or, we are firefighters.)

G, my name is Grace. My friend's name is George. We come from Green River, Utah. We sell grapes. (Or, we work at the garage fixing cars.)

H, my name is Harriet. My friend's name is Harry. We come from Hazard, Kentucky. We sell handlebars. (Or, we work at the hospital.)

I, my name is Ira. My friend's name is Iris. We come from Independence, Kansas. We sell ice cream. (Or, we are insurance agents.)

J, my name is Jack. My friend's name is Jake. We come from Jamestown, North Dakota. We sell jeans. (Or, we are jewelers.)

K, my name is Kelly. My friend's name is Ken. We come from Kalamazoo, Michigan. We sell kites. (Or, we take care of dogs at our kennel, or we are karate teachers.)

L, my name is Laura. My friend's name is Len. We come from Loveland, Colorado. We sell licorice. (Or, I am a librarian and Len is a lawyer.)

M, my name is Michael. My friend's name is Minnie. We come from Marshalltown, Iowa. We sell milk. (Or, we work at the market or mall or movie house or medical center.)

N, my name is Nicolas. My friend's name is Nancy. We come from New Bedford, Massachusetts. We sell nuts. (Or, we are newspaper reporters.)

O, my name is Olivia. My friend's name is Oscar. We come from Oshkosh, Wisconsin. We sell oatmeal. (Or, we are optometrists.)

P, my name is Paige. My friend's name is Pete. We come from Pine Bluff, Arkansas. We sell pumpkins. (Or, I am a policewoman and Pete is a plumber.)

Q, my name is Queenie. My friend's name is Quenton. We come from Quincy, Illinois. We sell quilts. (Or, we work at a quarry.)

R, my name is Robin. My friend's name is Roberto. We come from Riverside, California. We sell raisins. (Or, I work at the radio station and Roberto is a realtor or is a chef at a restaurant.)

S, my name is Sam. My friend's name is Spencer. We come from Sundance, Wyoming. We sell soup. (Or, work at a school or swimming pool.)

T, my name is Theodora. My friend's name is Ted. We come from Thief River Falls, Minnesota. We sell tacos. (Or, we are teachers.)

U, my name is Ulises. My friend's name is Ursula. We come from University Park, New Mexico. We sell unicorns. (Or, we own a uniform-supply shop.)

V, my name is Victoria. My friend's name is Vance. We come from Valentine, Nebraska. We sell vans. (We are veterinarians.)

W, my name is Wilma. My friend's name is Wilbur. We come from Walla, Walla, Washington. We sell whistles. (Or, we report the weather, or work at the weather station.)

X, my name is Xena. My friend's name is Xavier. We come from Xenia, Ohio. We sell xebecs. (Or, we are technicians at an X-ray laboratory.)

Y, my name is Yancy. My friend's name is Yolanda. We come from Yukon, Oklahoma. We sell yo yos. (Or, we are yoga instructors.)

Z, my name is Zelda. My friend's name is Zac. We come from Zapata, Texas. We sell zebras. (Or, we are zoologists at the zoo, or we work at the zoning department.)

Books about growing, change, identity, community

How Many Teeth by Paul Showers. Harper Trophy, 1991.

I Know a Lady by Charlotte Zolotow. William Morrow, 1984.

The Important Book by Margaret Wise Brown. Harper Trophy, 1977.

Me on the Map by Joan Sweeney. Crown, 1996.

My Place in Space by Robin and Sally Hirst. Five Mile Press, 1988.

New Shoes for Silvia by Johanna Hurwitz. William Morrow, 1993.

Newsman Ned Meets the New Family by Steven Kroll. Scholastic, 1988.

Once Upon a Time I Used to Be Older by Barbara Harmeyer. St. Martins Press, 1987.

The Scrambled States of the United States by Laurie Keller. Henry Holt, 1998.

Wilfrid Gordon McDonald Partridge by Mem Fox. Kane-Miller, 1984.

Alphabet books

Animalia by Graeme Base. Harry N. Abrams, 1986.

A My Name Is Alice by Jane Bayer. Penguin, 1984.

A to Zen by Ruth Wells. Picture Book Studio, 1992.

A Is for Africa by Ifeoma Onyefulu. Penguin, 1993.

A, My Name Is... by Alice Lyne. Whispering Coyote Press, 1997.

A Was Once an Apple Pie by Edward Lear. Candlewick, 1992.

The ABC Mystery by Doug Cushman. HarperCollins, 1993.

The Accidental Zucchini by Max Grover. Harcourt Brace, 1993.

All in the Woodland Early by Jane Yolen. Boyds Mill Press, 1997.

Alligator Arrived with Apples by Crescent Dragonwagon. Aladdin, 1987.

The Alphabet Tree by Leo Lionnl. Alfred Al Knopf, 1968.

Alphabet City by Stephen T. Johnson. Penguin, 1995.

The Alphabet from Z to A by Judith Viorst. Aladdin, 1994.

Chicka Chicka Boom Boom by Bill Martin. Simon & Schuster, 1989.

Eating the Alphabet by Lois Ehlert. Harcourt Brace Jovanovich, 1989.

The Icky Bug Alphabet Book by Jerry Pallotta. Charlesbridge, 1986.

On the River ABC by Caroline Stutson. Roberts Rinehart Publishers, 1993.

Potluck by Anne Shelby. Orchard, 1991.

Roger Tory Peterson's ABC of Birds by Linda Westervelt. Universe Publishing, 1995.

Tomorrow's Alphabet by George Shannon. William Morrow, 1996.

I Am Growing

We are writing a book about growing. Please think about some changes that have happened to you over the past six years. Write them down on the lines below by finishing the sentences.

When I was one

I could _____.

I wanted to _____.

When I was two

I could _____.

I wanted to _____.

When I was three

I could _____.

I wanted to _____.

When I was four

I could _____.

I wanted to _____.

When I was five

I could _____.

I wanted to _____.

When I was six

I could _____.

I wanted to _____.

Teaching Second Grade Scholastic

Designing a Cover

Use the blank paper attached to design your cover. It's your rough draft.

Where will you write the title?

A-Z U.S.A. Communities

Where will you write the author's name?

By _____
(your name)

Where will you glue the map?

Cut this map out and glue it to your rough draft cover design.

*Hint: You may want to use a ruler.

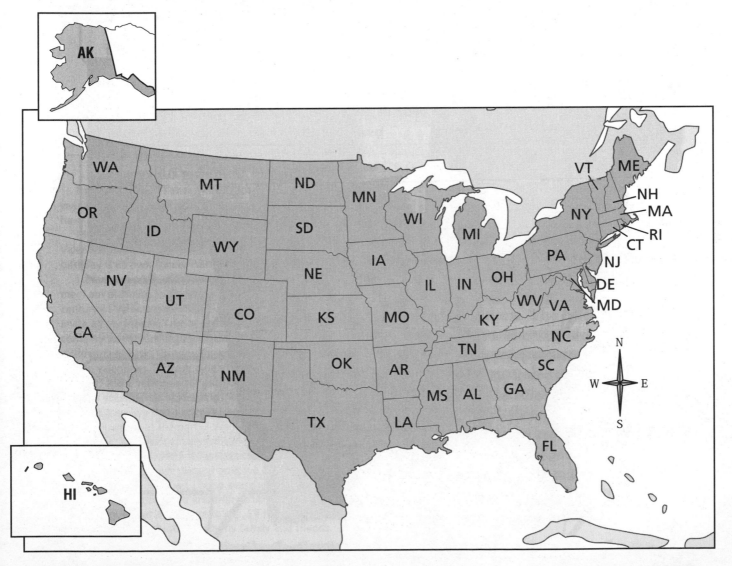

CHAPTER 12

Integrations

Integrating is taking a theme or unit of study across the curriculum areas. This is accomplished by finding ways to link reading, writing, math, science, and social studies with a unifying focus. Curriculum can be integrated by presenting a unit, theme, activity, and/or projects that address more than one discipline at a time. In other words, an activity may focus on learning and using math skills but enable students to acquire social studies knowledge as well. Second graders, who are lively and eager to learn, love integrated studies.

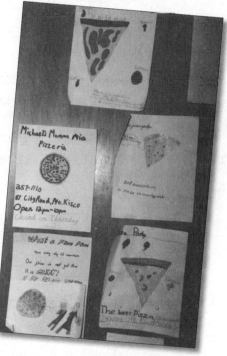

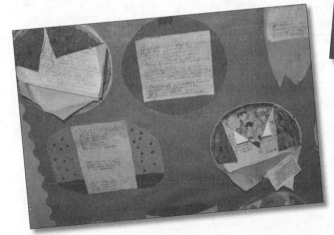

Why integrate curriculum?

Math, science, and social studies integrations initiate learning connections needed for a lifetime learner, and integrating curriculum is a natural way to present information to your class. After all, when we go shopping, we don't say to ourselves, "Oh, it's time for me to do math." (How much of each item do I need to make this recipe?) Or, "Oh, it's time for geography." (Do you prefer Washington State apples or New York State apples?) Or, "Oh it's time for me to do science." (It's 90 degrees outside. Can I get this ice cream home before it melts?)

Even though you may not stop and tell your class, "It's math time," it is important to emphasize each of the curriculum areas and not depend only on reading to do that for you. For example, you might read a story or two about quilts, and these stories might include patterns, sorting, and design ideas. But simply reading the story and looking at the designs is not enough. You need to apply these ideas to hands-on classroom projects—perhaps having students create quilt designs out of paper.

How can an integration be designed?

Using a graphic organizer (see page 173) is very helpful. It directs attention across curriculum areas as you gather materials and research and begin to develop ideas. Once you choose a theme based on interest or curriculum, fill in the graphic organizer with the activities. By the way, some of the best ideas come from the children in your class as they make connections and ask questions. There's always room for change and improvement.

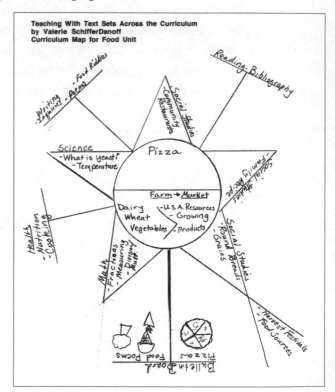

Teaching With Text Sets Across the Curriculum
by Valerie SchifferDanoff
Curriculum Map for Food Unit

What are good ways to locate appropriate books for the theme?

Once you've chosen a theme or unit of study, begin by reading books. It's especially easy to look up books by subject in a computer-based library or bookstore on the Internet (Amazon.com), or a catalog from a publishing company like Scholastic. Determine whether the books are at an appropriate level for second grade by looking at the amount of text on each page and at the illustrations. Sort the books by fiction and nonfiction; large-group shared reading and independent or small-group reading; and science, social studies, and math focus.

What are some ways to develop projects and activities?

There are lots of teacher resources filled with project ideas, themes, and literature responses. (See a resource list at the end of this chapter for the food integration described in this chapter.) Look through these and find ideas that can work with the theme or unit of study. To design your own, it's helpful to use a model. If you're creating a pop-up book, consult a pop-up book for construction ideas. For a favorite trade book, children can rewrite their own version. A shape book can be created for almost any subject by using the outside perimeter of an object to determine the shape. You can enlarge the shape on a copy machine or by using an overhead projector.

The types of activities you do will depend on the theme. However, generally science lends itself to observations and experiments; social studies to mapping, interviews, and cultural sharing; math to applications and extensions of skills; writing to poetry, research, and writing their own version; and reading to reading fiction and nonfiction on the subject. A concluding celebration might be a theme-based party, a field trip, a walk, guest speakers, book sharing, or a special snack. You can use the following integration about food as a model for integration of other subjects.

Food Integration

Pizza is the focus of this integration, and its purpose is to help children understand that the production of food is interdependent, that it is a farm-to-market process, that the three types of communities—rural, suburban, and urban—are all part of the process, and that communities are people and families with traditions that include food.

An integration like this enables children to discover that each curriculum area plays a role. Looking at the graphic organizer and the lessons described below, you'll get an idea of how the activities are integrated into the curriculum areas:

- **Social Studies**: concepts of interdependence, farm to market, family, traditional foods
- **Math:** fractions, measurement, temperature, graphing
- **Science**: temperature, observation
- **Health/Science:** observation, nutrition, cooking
- **Reading:** nonfiction, fiction

- **Writing:** journal, inquiry-based, riddles, poetry
- **Art:** pop-up books, bulletin board
- **Culminating Activity:** food-sharing luncheon

The lessons are numbered. However, because an integration covers the whole curriculum, more than one lesson will be given on a day. For instance, in the morning children may read books about pizza and work on a reading response. Later that morning there might be a related math activity, while in the afternoon the integration continues with inquiry-based writing. An integration like this can take four to six weeks.

Language Arts

LESSON 1 **GETTING STARTED: LARGE-GROUP SHARED READING**

Reading a book is always a motivating way to start a unit of study. *How My Family Lives in America* by Susan Kuklin (Simon & Schuster, 1992) can set the scene for the study of food. However, many of the other suggested books can also initiate the study of food. (See page 172.) The Kuklin book is about four different families, their cultural or traditional foods, and the American foods they like to eat. One of the families enjoys pizza, which becomes the main focus of this integration.

After reading the story, discuss the kinds of foods the children in your class eat at home. Then...

1 Challenge your class with this riddle:

> We're going to study something you love.
> It's something we cannot live without.
> You need to have it every day.

(Allow them to guess. Then continue by telling a riddle about your focus food.)

> It's round.
> It's eaten hot.
> It can have toppings.

2 Once your students guess pizza, continue by having them set up a KWL page in their journals with a heading that reads "What I know about pizza" and another that reads "What I want to know about pizza." Then have them list anything they may know about pizza and anything they might want to know about pizza under those headings. ⓗ This can be a homework assignment. A child asked, "Where do the bubbles come from?" This was answered with the yeast experiment on page 165.

LESSON 2 SHARING JOURNAL WRITING

Children enjoy sharing what they know and what they want to know. Allow for some time to do this before beginning the small-group reading and inquiry-based writing. The children will soon discover the answers to some of their questions and you will find out what the class does know about pizza.

LESSON 3 SMALL-GROUP READING

If you can't gather enough books for small-group or individual reading, the whole integration can be done with large-group shared reading and individual responses.

How Pizza Came to Queens by Dayal Kaur Khalsa (Random House, 1979), *Little Nino's Pizzeria* by Karen Barbour (Harcourt Brace Jovanovich, 1987), *The Pizza War* by Mercer Mayer (Western Publishing Co., 1995), and *The Pizza Book* by Stephen Krensky (Scholastic, 1992) are books well suited for small-group reading. Within each of these books, whether fiction or nonfiction, the children will learn the ingredients of pizza and how pizza is made. For a reading response, instruct children to write a list of pizza ingredients and directions for making a pizza by extrapolating the needed information and rewriting it in their own words.

Over the next few days, have the children take turns reading each of the books, writing how each answers the questions about making pizza and pizza ingredients, and comparing what they've learned from each. Check for readability of each text and assign paired reading if necessary.

Each child chooses the response he or she likes best, types it on the computer, and makes a hard copy to glue onto one of the slices of the pizza pop-up book they'll be creating. (See page 161.)

Math

LESSON 1   INTRODUCING FRACTIONS

MATERIALS NEEDED FOR EACH CHILD

- crackers that are perforated in quarters
- fraction manipulative materials: whole, halves, and quarters
- fraction circle paper (See page 174.)
- fraction homework paper (See page 175.)
- precut circles in three colors of construction paper
- scissors, glue, colored pencils

1 Be sure the children have all the materials at their desks or tables.

2 For a read aloud, use all or part of one of the following books: *Fraction Fun* by David A. Adler (Holiday House, 1996), *Fraction Action* by Loreen Leedy (Holiday House, 1994), *Eating Fractions* by Bruce McMillan (Scholastic, 1991). I recommend the first part of each of the first two books or all of the last. Hand out the perforated crackers and have the children break them into halves and quarters.

3 Use a clock transparency on an overhead projector. Review half and quarter past. (Since the clock is a circle divided into quarters and halves, and you may have already taught about clocks and time, you can help the children make a connection.) Replace the clock circle with a plain circle on the overhead. Demonstrate how to divide that circle. Name and shade in the fractions quarter and half.

4 Direct the children to their seats and direct their attention to the clock pattern on their paper. Have them place the circle template on the clock. Then have them place the half circle. Continue with one quarter, being sure the children grasp the relationship between the vocabulary and the actual measure.

5 Continue by directing the children to place whole, halves, and quarters on top of the plain circle below the clock.

6 Call the children's attention to the precut paper circles. You might relate the shape to food. Tell a story of wanting to share a cookie equally with one friend. Have the children pretend the brown circle is the cookie. Ask, "What would you need to do?" "Break it in half!" is the answer you want. Respond with,

- This is paper, how can we make two halves?
- Cut it!
- How can we cut it to make it equal?

They may say "Down the middle" or "Fold it in half." "Fold it in half," is what you're looking for to continue. Then have the children fold the paper in half and then unfold it and cut along the fold line. Next, have them glue one half onto the circle below the clock. Put the extra half aside for now.

7 Now direct the children to pick up another colored circle. Again you can pretend this is a food item, maybe a lemon tart. Say that you want to share your tart with three friends, which means you now need four pieces all together. Repeat the above to get to halves. Then continue by folding and cutting each half in half to make quarters. Glue the quarters onto the circle next to the clock.

8 Direct the children to place one half and two quarters in the circle below that. Say the words and have them repeat that "one half equals two quarters." Then have them cut another circle into quarters. Have them glue the half that they put aside on one side of the circle and two of the quarters on the other side of the circle.

9 Next to the four-quarters circle, have the children glue down the other two quarters opposite each other to create a pattern.

10 On the last circle have the children trace the manipulative materials to divide the circle in half on one side and into quarters on the other side. Teach them how to write one half and one quarter. Have them label this last circle correctly and gently shade in each fraction with a colored pencil.

H Hand out the homework paper and go over directions for completion.

LESSON 2 REINFORCING FRACTIONS

1 Have the children trace the whole-circle manipulative on white paper.

2 Using half, quarter, third, and sixth manipulative materials, instruct them to color and label halves, quarters, thirds, and sixths. Model the process on a chart.

LESSON 3 MAKING A PIZZA POP-UP BOOK AND REINFORCING FRACTION SKILLS

MATERIALS

- ◎ tagboard circle template (12"–14" in diameter)
- ◎ 2 pieces of 14" x 14" tag board, per child
- ◎ 1 piece of string/child
- ◎ ruler
- ◎ scissors, glue, pencil, markers, crayons or colored pencils

1 Tell the children they're going to use their fraction skills to make a pizza pop- up book.

2 Hold up the circle template (pizza blank). Review the concepts of halves, quarters, and thirds. Instruct the children to trace around the circle onto one piece of the tag board, then cut around the whole circle. This will be the back cover of their book.

3 Have the children trace this circle onto the other piece of tag board and cut it out to use for the front cover.

4 Model and have the children lay their string across the blank circle (front cover) and trim it to size. Then have them fold the string in half, and cut it at the fold to make two equal pieces of string (each being the radius of the circle).

5 Model and instruct children to place one end of the string on the outer edge of the circle going into the center to determine center. Mark the center with a pencil.

6 Have the children use rulers to draw a line dividing the circle in half. (They can check by making a light fold.) Then have them divide the halves into quarters. Have children label these fractions.

Assessment Tip
Assess understanding and reinforce skills as students make the covers by asking:

How many halves are there in a whole?

How many quarters are there in a whole? in a half?

How many eighths are there in a whole? in a quarter? in a half?

Have the children color the front, cover to look like their favorite pizza. Once it's colored, have the children cut this into fourths according to the markings. Have them lay the fourths on top of the blank side of the back cover and glue just the outer round edges to the outer edge of the blank side of the back cover. Allow the pizzas to dry. Then the children can fold each fourth back to create a pizza pop-up cover.

The pizza pop-up can display all the work your students have completed for this integration. Staple the reading responses each child chose to type on the computer to the middle of the top of the back cover. Each of the four pieces of pizza (folded back) can hold another learning piece: recipe for pizza, list of pizzerias, list titled "Round Breads Around the World," pizza poem.

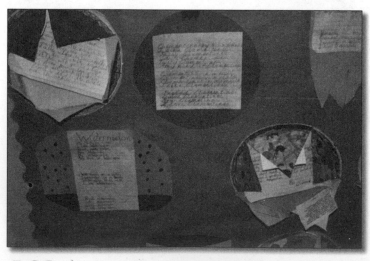

LESSON 4 GRAPHING/CHARTING

MATERIALS

⊙ 1 copy of survey paper (See page 36.)

⊙ 1 piece of graph paper

1 Using survey paper, ask the children: What are your favorite pizza toppings?

2 Take the survey.

3 Have children transfer the information to individual graphs and color for a bar graph display.

As an extension activity, you may want to ask about their favorite vegetable, favorite dairy product, favorite beverage to drink with pizza, favorite food.

Social Studies

LESSONS 1, 2, 3

INQUIRY-BASED, LARGE-GROUP SHARED READING AND WRITING

Tell your class that now they're going to begin answering some of their questions about pizza. You'll be reading books that tell about the ingredients, where pizzas originate, how they're produced, and how the ingredients get to you in the form of a pizza.

1 Read *From Grain to Bread* by Ali Mitgutsch (Carolrhoda, 1997). On a chart write the facts the children learned from the book as they volunteer them.

2 Have the children copy the facts onto composition paper that has been cut to size to fit inside pizza pop-up cover.

Repeat above for Lessons 2 and 3 reading *Vegetables, Vegetables!* by Fay Robinson (Children's Book Press, 1994) and *Milk from Cow to Carton* by Aliki (HarperCollins, 1992).

Pizza is made from...
fruits and vegetables.
Fruits and vegetables are plants.
Fruits have seeds.
Vegetables are bulbs, flowers, roots or leaf parts of plants.
Vegetables and fruits are grown on a farm.
Most of our vegetables and fruits in the U.S.A. are grown in California and Florida.
Fruits and vegetables are transported to factories, markets and pizzerias.

A Week of Pizza Homework

Lessons 1 through 5 give the children reading and math practice and expand their text knowledge and use.

MATERIALS

- local phone book
- 2 pieces white writing paper
- 1 piece composition paper

LESSON 1 LOOKING IN THE PHONE BOOK

1 Show the children ads for pizzerias in the phone book.

2 Instruct the children to find ads for pizzerias in their phone books at home and write down names of pizzerias and the towns in which they're located.

LESSON 2 CREATING PIZZERIA ADS

1 Check and discuss homework. Put it aside to be typed for the pizza pop-up.

2 Hand out pieces of plain white paper. Instruct the children to design an ad for their own pizza restaurant. Remind them of what was included in the phone-book ads—name of restaurant, pictures, addresses, phone numbers, specialties, and so on. They can use colored pencils for added effect.

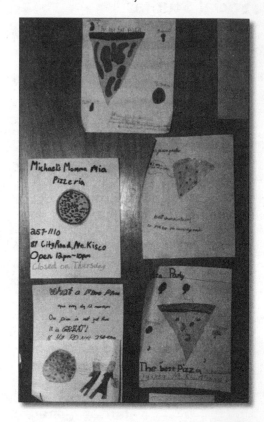

LESSON 3 MAKING A MENU

1 Show students copies of pizzeria menus.

2 Instruct children to make a menu for their restaurant. Tell them to keep prices to a reasonable sum, as these prices will be used to write story problems the next day.

LESSON 4   MENU MATH

1 Share the children's menus.

2 Give examples of story problems using a menu.

3 Have the children use their menus to write story problems.

LESSON 5   SHARING STORY PROBLEMS

Share story problems in class.

Science

LESSON 1   YEAST EXPERIMENT

Children absolutely love this experiment.

MATERIALS

- ◎ 3 packets of dry yeast for each pair of children
- ◎ self-sealing sandwich bags
- ◎ 3 thermometers for each pair of children, plus extra thermometers
- ◎ access to water of 110–120°F
- ◎ beakers to hold the water
- ◎ scissors
- ◎ sugar

1 Prepare three beakers with water of different temperatures. Place the thermometers in the water allowing children to view and observe the different temperatures.

2 Discuss with children that yeast is a living organism and that it wakes up in water of about 110 degrees.

3 Pair the children. Hand out self-sealing bags, yeast packets, scissors. Have each pair cut open their yeast packets and pour the yeast into the bags.

4 Have each pair measure $\frac{1}{2}$ teaspoon sugar and then $\frac{1}{4}$ cup 110-degree water into their bags.

5 Check the bags every 15 minutes for about one hour. Have the children record their observations in their individual journals and/or on a class chart.

6 Explain and discuss that while yeast looks just like a powder, it is a living organism. Like the mushroom that goes on the pizza, yeast is a kind of

fungus, a plant. Green plants make their own food. A fungus must live on other foods. Like most living things, yeast needs water to live. The warm water wakes the yeast up and then the yeast uses the sugar for its food. The yeast feeds on the sugar. It takes energy from the sugar, and breaks it down into alcohol plus a gas called carbon dioxide. That's why the ziplock bags puff up. When yeast is used in dough, the escaping carbon dioxide is what causes the dough to rise. These bubbles are the bubbles we often see on the crust on the pizza. While the yeast may smell unpleasant during the experiment, it gives bread its delicious smell while baking.

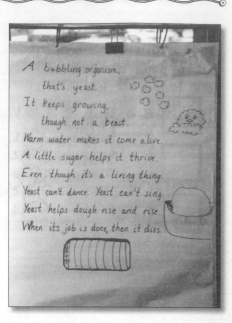

A bubbling organism,
   that's yeast.
It keeps growing,
   though not a beast.
Warm water makes it come alive.
A little sugar helps it thrive.
Even though it's a living thing,
Yeast can't dance. Yeast can't sing.
Yeast helps dough rise and rise.
When its job is done, then it dies.

Assessment Tip

Assess by having children write in their journals what they learned about yeast. Look for key points:

Yeast is a living thing.

Like most living things, it needs water.

Warm water wakes it up.

Yeast feeds on sugar.

Yeast gives off a gas or carbon dioxide.

That's what makes dough rise.

LESSON 2   COOKING

Now it's time to put it all together by cooking pizza and enjoying everything you've been reading and discussing about this favorite food. You can do this by simply making round-bread pizzas (with bagels, pita, muffins, chapati, and so on), making a pizza from scratch, or both.

1 Discuss that pizza is a round bread.

2 Brainstorm a list of round breads.

3 List on a chart other ingredients needed to make pizza.

4 Assign each child either bread, cheese, or sauce to bring into

school. If necessary, arrange for a few parent volunteers to help make the pizza.

Hint: Hopefully you'll have a volunteer that has made pizza before. Otherwise look for a simple recipe in a pizza cookbook and try it out at home first. A pizza round is very easy to make.

Writing

LESSON 1   PIZZA POEM

Now that children have learned about and tasted pizza, they are ready to write a simple pizza poem. If you're using poetry journals, have children write their poem there. Then edit, type, and glue it onto one slice of the pizza pop-up.

1   Tell the children they're going to write a poem about pizza. Remind them about its ingredients, taste, smell, feel, and so on.

2   To create a list poem, model on a chart the words "Pizza is..." Then list descriptive words. Brainstorm more words with the children. They'll quickly get the idea. Limiting this poem to a list guarantees success. The list words can range from one word on a line to three. For example,

> Pizza is...
>> hot
>> gooey
>> chewy
>> soft and hard
>> bubbly
>> cheesy
>> stringy
>> saucy
>> spicy
>> delicious
>> my favorite food!

> **Assessment Tip**
> Assess learning by having children write in their journals: "What I learned about pizza" to complete their KWL charts. Then discuss other foods that are made from grain, dairy, fruit, and vegetables. Further reading reinforces, transfers, and assesses learning.

Extending the food unit

Certainly stopping with pizza can be enough. However, extending with more food books reinforces and assesses the learning. Children easily inquire about other grains, dairy products, and produce. They now have a sense of the resources from which these foods are produced. Continue the study with the books on the lists, or try some of the following activities.

Reading

LESSON 1   READING AND WRITING A RIDDLE

MATERIALS

- 12" x 18" construction paper
- composition paper
- a thin black marker
- colored pencils, crayons, or markers

Second graders love riddles! Riddles written in this format make a great bulletin board display. Either read or tell some riddles. *What Food Is This?* by Rosmarie Hauserr (Scholastic, 1995) is just right for a large-group, small-group, or whole-class read. Reading it is a great way to bridge or extend from pizza to other foods. Use the format below to model writing a riddle. Then have each child choose a food and use the format to write his or her own riddle.

1 Write a riddle on composition paper using two lines so the letters are large. Go over the letters in black thin-line marker so the riddle will show up from a distance.

2 Glue the riddle onto one edge of 12" x 18" construction paper (see photo) so that the other side can be folded toward the composition paper to hide the answer.

3 Draw clues on top of the folded edge. Write the answer and draw a picture of the food inside.

4 Once children have completed their riddles, allow time for sharing before they are displayed on the bulletin board.

LESSON 2   VENN DIAGRAM

Mouse Trap by Joy Cowley (Scholastic, 1995), *Mouse Soup* by Arnold Lobel (Harper Trophy, 1977), and *Too Many Babas* by Carolyn Croll (Harper Trophy, 1979) are books that second graders read and enjoy comparing.

- *Mouse Trap* is about mice that avoid the cat's trap while looking for cheese.

- *Mouse Soup* is about a mouse who is captured by a weasel who wants to use the mouse as a main ingredient for his soup. The mouse convinces the weasel that he needs more ingredients, telling a tale about each ingredient. The weasel goes to find the ingredients and the mouse escapes.

- ⦿ *Too Many Babas* is an endearing story that basically illustrates how "too many cooks spoil the broth." In the end the babas work cooperatively to make the soup again.

Children can read two of these books independently. *Mouse Trap* can be compared to *Mouse Soup* since each involves a trap. *Mouse Soup* can be compared to *Too Many Babas* since each involves cooking soup. Be sure to meet with groups of children for book talks to discuss comparisons and contrasts.

Then give each child a copy of a Venn diagram to fill in. Children can work with you in pairs or groups. (For more on Venn diagrams see Reading Responses, page 46.)

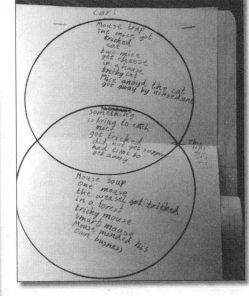

Writing

. . . .

LESSON 1   FOOD POEMS

If you choose to extend this study to include other foods, you might have the children write a food poem, then create a representation and paste the poem to it for display. Adding these to the pizza bulletin board gives it a nice flavor.

A pattern poem is also a quick success.

1 Ask children to define a pattern (something that repeats itself).

2 Tell them that they're going to write a pattern poem about their most or least favorite food.

3 Model the process by writing your own pattern poem.

Prewrite the pattern on chart paper or using an overhead, leaving spaces blank.

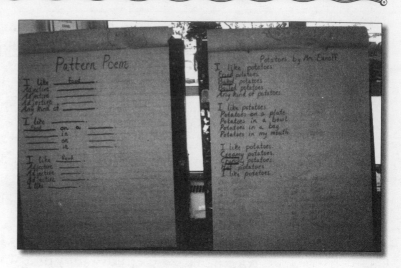

Pattern:

I like _____
Adjective _____
Adjective _____
Adjective _____
Any kind of _____

I like _____
_____ prepositional phrase
_____ prepositional phrase
_____ prepositional phrase

I like _____
Adjective _____
Adjective _____
Adjective _____
I like _____

A poem may look like:

I like potatoes.
Creamy potatoes,
Crunchy potatoes,
Baked potatoes,
Any kind of potatoes.

I like potatoes.
Potatoes on a plate.
Potatoes in a bowl.
Potatoes in my mouth.

I like potatoes.
Cold potatoes.
Fried potatoes.
Hash brown potatoes.
I like potatoes.

Place the poem on construction paper and draw a representation of the food around it. Then color it with markers where appropriate. Glue the poem onto the construction paper after the paper is cut.

LESSON 2   IMAGINATION STATION FLIP BOOK

This project begins with a very funny flip book, *Ketchup On Your Cornflakes?* by Nick Sharratt (Scholastic, 1994). The pages mix and match, creating different funny food combinations. I set this project up in my Imagination Station.

MATERIALS

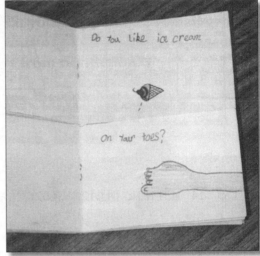

- ◎ lightweight tag board for covers
- ◎ white construction paper for pages
- ◎ stapler
- ◎ crayon, markers, or colored pencils
- ◎ sentence strips
- ◎ chart paper

1 To make a sample book to share with the class, cut the construction paper and tag board to 9½" x 6½".

2 Fold the covers and pages in half and staple them together at the edge. If you have a long-arm stapler, you can staple the inside center to fold like a book.

3 Cut the pages in half, leaving about a half-inch margin to keep book intact. Pages can be folded back to allow for flipping.

4 Write directions for your students on sentence strips on chart paper.

5 Read *Ketchup On Your Cornflakes?* to your class.

6 Share your sample book.

7 Read over the directions with the children.

8 Have the children work on this project independently. You may want to brainstorm with them to choose a food and to give them ideas.

Hint: Keep a word chart nearby for correct spelling. Also have children write words in pencil in case corrections are needed before they go over them in ink to create the finished books.

Celebration

Encourage children to find out about their family culture and traditional foods.

Hopefully, the children have been commenting about this during their adventures with food. Finally, celebrate with a Food, Glorious Food! luncheon. Involving more than one class at the same grade level makes the celebration an even greater success.

Books about food

Fiction

1000 Silly Sandwiches by Alan Benjamin. Simon & Schuster, 1995.

The Biggest Sandwich Ever by Rita Golden Gelman. Scholastic, 1980.

Chato's Kitchen by Gary Soto. The Putnam Grossett Group, 1995.

Everybody Cooks Rice by Norah Dooley. Carolrhoda, 1991.

Frannie's Fruits by Leslie Kimmelman. Harper & Row, 1989.

How to Eat Fried Worms by Thomas Rockwell. Bantam, 1973.

How Pizza Came to Queens by Dayal Kaur Khalsa. Random House, 1979.

Jalapeno Bagels by Natasha Wing. Simon & Schuster, 1996.

A Job for Wittilda by Carolyn and Mark Buehner. Penguin, 1993.

Just Us Women by Jeannette Caines. Harper & Row, 1982.

Ketchup on Your Cornflakes? by Nick Sharratt. Scholastic, 1994.

The King of Pizza by Sylvester Sanzari. Workman Publishing, 1995.

Little Nino's Pizzeria by Karen Barbour. Harcourt Brace Jovanovich, 1987.

Mouse Trap by Joy Cowley. Scholastic, 1995.

Mouse Soup by Arnold Lobel. Harper Trophy, 1977.

Pete's a Pizza by William Steig. HarperCollins, 1998.

Pizza Pat by Rita Golden Gelman. Random House, 1999.

The Pizza War by Mercer Mayer. Western Publishing Co, 1995.

The Rattlebang Picnic by Margaret Mahy. Penguin, 1994.

Strega Nona by Tomie dePaola. Prentice Hall, 1975.

This is the Way We Eat Our Lunch by Edith Baer. Scholastic, 1995.

Too Many Babas by Carolyn Croll. Harper Trophy, 1979.

Too Many Tamales by Gary Soto. Putnam & Grossett, 1993.

Tops and Bottoms by Janet Stevens. Harcourt Brace, 1995.

Nonfiction

Bread, Bread, Bread by Ann Morris. William Morrow, 1989.

Cow by Jules Older. Charlesbridge, 1997.

Dairy Products Farm to Market by Jason Cooper. Rourke Publications, 1997.

Day in the Life of a Chef by Miriam Anne Bourn. Troll, 1988.

From Milk to Ice Cream by Ali Mitgutsch. Carolrhoda Books, 1979.

From Grain to Bread by Ali Mitgutsch. Carolrhoda, 1971.

Harvest Year by C. Peterson. Boyds Mills, 1996.

How My Family Lives in America by Susan Kuklin. Simon & Schuster, 1992.

Let's Find Out About Ice Cream by Mary Ebeltoft Reid. Scholastic, 1996.

Make Me a Peanut Butter Sandwich by Ken Robbins. Scholastic, 1992.

Many Friends Cooking by Terry Touff Cooper and Marilyn Ratner. Philomel, 1980.

Milk from Cow to Carton by Aliki. HarperCollins, 1992.

Pizza Book by Stephen Krensky. Scholastic, 1992.

Pizza Cookbook by Myra Street. Quintet Publishing, 1995.

Pizza! by (Real Reading) by Franklin W. Dixon. Steck-Vaughn, 1998.

This Is the Way We Eat Our Lunch by Edith Baer. Scholastic, 1995.

Vegetables, Vegetables! by Fay Robinson. Children's Press, 1994.

What Food is This? by Rosmarie Hausherr. Scholastic, 1995.

Math

10 for Dinner by Jo Ellen Bogart. Scholastic, 1989.

Eating Fractions by Bruce McMillan. Scholastic, 1991.

Fraction Action by Loreen Leedy. Holiday House, 1994.

Fraction Fun by David A. Adler. Holiday House, 1996.

My Little Sister Ate One Hare by Bill Grossman. Crown, 1996.

Graphic Organizer

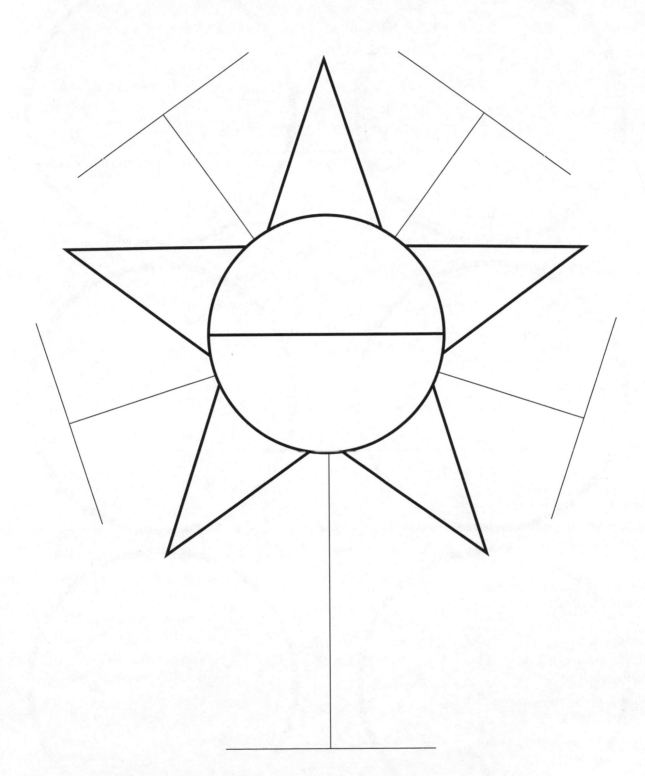

Fraction Circles

Equal Parts: Halves and Quarters

Color and complete.

$\frac{1}{2}$ red

$\frac{1}{2}$ blue

$\frac{1}{4}$ orange

$\frac{1}{4}$ blue and $\frac{1}{4}$ red

$\frac{1}{4}$ yellow, $\frac{1}{4}$ blue and $\frac{1}{4}$ red

$\frac{1}{4}$ yellow, $\frac{1}{4}$ blue, $\frac{1}{4}$ red, $\frac{1}{4}$ green

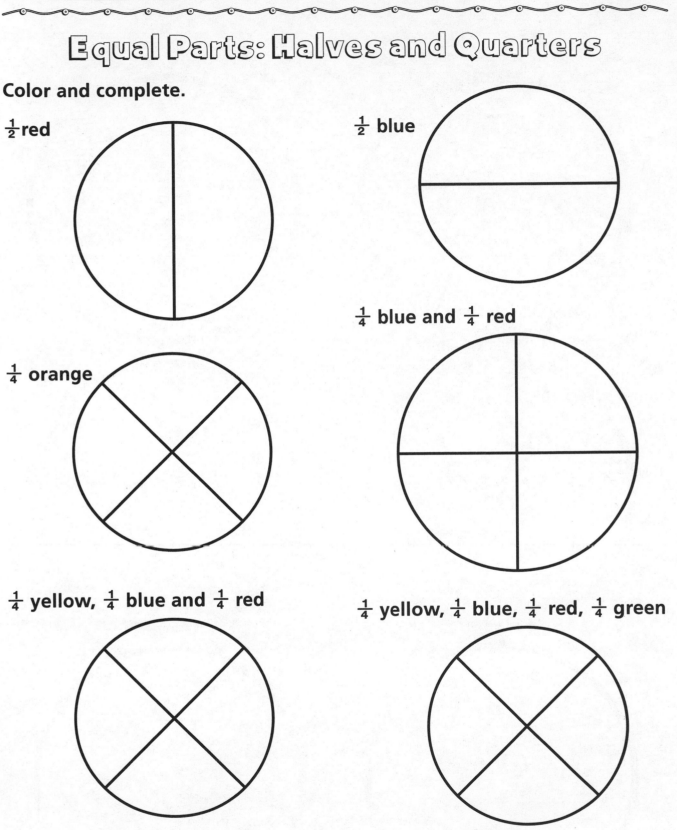

Find a square or circle at home. Trace it on a piece of paper. Divide it into two equal parts. Trace it again. Then divide it into four equal parts. Color each part a different color.